John Pritchard is Bishop of Jarrov
Canterbury and, before that, Warden of Cranmer Hall, Durham.
He has served in parishes in Birmingham and Taunton and has
been Diocesan Youth Officer for Bath and Wells diocese. Previous
books by the author include *The Intercessions Handbook*,
Beginning Again, *Living the Gospel Stories Today* and *How to
Pray*. He is married with two daughters.

LEADING
INTERCESSIONS

Creative ideas for public
and private prayer

JOHN PRITCHARD

First published in Great Britain in 2004 by
The Society for Promoting Christian Knowledge (SPCK)
under the title *The Second Intercessions Handbook:*
More creative ideas for public and private prayer

Published in the United States of America and Canada by the
Liturgical Press, Saint John's Abbey, Collegeville, Minnesota 56321-7500
www.litpress.org

Library of Congress Control Number: 2004113528

ISBN 0–8146–1827–8

10 9 8 7 6 5 4 3 2 1

Printed in Great Britain

CONTENTS

A WORD AT THE BEGINNING

I'm very glad you've found this book and I hope you find it helpful. It follows on from *The Intercessions Handbook,* which was an attempt to broaden the imaginative range of the intercessions we use in public worship, in small groups and in personal prayer.

In the years since the first book was published I've been encouraged by the intercessions I've encountered. I sense that as a Church we're giving more attention to this aspect of our relationship with God. But the demand for more help, with more ideas and different approaches, continues. Hence this follow-up volume.

Inevitably this book is integrally related to the first one. In other words, some of the principles and generic ideas are to be found in the first volume, and I've tried to avoid 'vain repetition'. On the other hand, this particular book has enough in it, I hope, to stimulate the happy reader into his or her own imaginative explorations of intercession.

This leads into the most important point of all: *please don't use these intercessions!* What I mean is, these intercessions are not meant to be used straight from the book – unless you and I, and your situation and my situation, are almost spookily the same! This is simply to recognize that these ways of interceding and these particular words are my own, and not yours. So please change them to make them fit your own situation and your own 'voice'.

The other main point I'd like to make here is that, although I've split the sections of this book up in a particular way, you may well find that an idea in, say, the section on Informal Worship and Small Groups might in your setting work well for a youth group or even in your mainstream service. Don't be tied down. Let the Spirit improvise! However, the sections I've chosen as a starting-point are these:

1 Mainstream worship
2 Festivals and special occasions
3 Informal worship and small groups
4 Children and young people
5 Personal prayer

Above all, enjoy the adventure of prayer! Let your heart and mind set sail for this glorious, colourful Creator, and see what kinds of prayer emerge. For what it's worth, my experience is that there's always far more to discover than we ever dreamed of.

Here are some of the beliefs about prayer which I hold to be true and which provide the context for the intercessions in this book:

– Intercession is one of the best ways we've got of loving someone. We can't do more for anyone than put them in the hands of a God who cares for them even more than we do. There are a few people I know who pray for me regularly each week and I'm more grateful for that gift than I can say.

– Intercession is not a matter of persuading God to do the right thing. Rather, it's taking hold of God's desire to do the best thing. It's taking hold of his willingness, not overcoming his reluctance.

– God is always there before us. We don't give him any new ideas when we pray, or introduce him to someone he doesn't already know and love to bits! We simply put our love and care at God's disposal.

– In the economy of God, our prayer helps to open a situation more fully to his love. And who knows what inexhaustible love can do? Jesus was always experimenting with divine love and seeing what it could achieve. In prayer we do the same. In any created universe there are bound to be limits to this, but as we don't know what they are, we can pray about everything and then leave the outcome to God working through the fabric of his own creation.

- God's love is a constant. He's always 'on our side'. He never changes his commitment to our well-being. Remember the litany 'God is good – all of the time. All of the time – God is good.' The evidence for that is the life of Jesus. Never be persuaded otherwise.

- 'Answers' to prayer aren't simply of the 'yes or no' variety. Prayer is a conversation in a relationship, and relationships are much more subtle, and our responses to each other much more nuanced than mere 'yes' or 'no'. Prayer isn't internet shopping!

- All prayer is 'answered' in the sense that all prayer is used by God in the best possible way. Our expression of desire in prayer may be misconceived but the loving intention is what really matters, and God will be able to take and use that for his good purposes.

- We don't pray and intercede out of our own boundless insight and wisdom! We are promised that the Spirit of God will pray in us. 'The Spirit intercedes for us with sighs too deep for words'(Romans 8.26). That takes the pressure off a bit!

I'm particularly grateful to my wife Wendy and to our special friend Ruth Etchells for splendidly perceptive improvements on the text. Liz Marsh and Alison Barr at SPCK have, as ever, been excellent editors to work with. But the faults and eccentricities are mine alone. The book stands or falls by whether it is valuable in helping us all to pray with serious joy and to place our hope afresh in the living God.

John Pritchard

1 INTERCESSIONS IN
MAINSTREAM WORSHIP

PRACTICALITIES

This is a checklist of things to consider when preparing
intercessions for mainstream worship:

1   **Decide what's special about this service.** Is there a main theme
from the Church's year or from local church life? Will it be a
solemn occasion or a less formal one? Any major events in the life
of the community or nation? What will be the mood of the
church in this service?

2   **Know your congregation.** What might be on people's minds?
What cultures are people coming from? What is the emotional
range people will be comfortable with?

3   **Pray about the real world and not a narrowly religious one.**
Demonstrate the connectedness between this one hour in church
and the 167 hours people won't be in church this week.

4   **Be particular.** Use examples from life, news reports, specific
people. Paint word pictures, use images. Avoid generalizations,
repetition and lists. But equally, don't be so specific that no one
else can identify with what you are praying for!

5   **Use vivid language.** Be rich and memorable in the language
you use, without being 'flowery'. A touch of quality – even poetry
– about our language can lift people's spirits in prayer.

6   **Have a clear structure.** Order and familiarity help. Responses
are good because they involve people, but they shouldn't be so

complex that people forget them. So, short responses, repeated at the start, or printed on the service sheet.

7   Address biddings to the people and prayers to God. The two are often confused! Bidding: 'We remember the dramatic scenes on our televisions last night . . .'. Prayer: 'Father, we pray for . . .'.

8   Pray: don't just read notes. Even if they are written out, the intention of the heart needs to be directed towards God, not the piece of paper!

9   Use silence, and take risks. Most people are longing for a bit more space and stillness in our worship, so give real time for prayer – don't panic after a few seconds of silence!

10   Use variety. Don't settle for one predictable form and shape. God is infinitely rich and colourful, and our prayers should reflect that depth and diversity.

11   Look for training and feedback. Ask for it if it isn't offered.

(1) LET US PRAY 1

The task facing thousands of people all over the country every Sunday is how to produce intercessions that are topical, crisp, comprehensive, down-to-earth, relevant – and if possible memorable and poetic! It's a tall order. Perhaps it's best to start by asking, 'What might we want to bring to God this week as our genuine concerns, hopes and fears?' Here is a possible approach, shaped around the common themes of church, world, community and those in need.

The response to the words 'Lord, hear us' is '**Lord, graciously hear us**'.

Gracious God, we bring to you the things we care most about this morning. Help us to be honest with what we bring. Hear the whisper of our hearts as well as the sound of our words.

Lord, hear us. **Lord, graciously hear us.**

We remember before you the glorious carnival of people who make up what we call 'the Church':

the hard-working bishop in Africa with little money, few priests and fragile administration, but huge faith, great love and infectious hope;

the wardens (deacons etc.), organists and treasurers on whom our churches depend, who come early and leave late, and somehow need to meet God for themselves in between; the loyal team who look after children's activities, even though they're tired after a week's work and need encouragement and thanks; the person new to church, puzzled but seeking, not sure if this is right for them, but here again anyway;

the people sitting and kneeling around us now – people to be cared for and prayed for as fellow members of this extraordinary family of God.

3

May your blessing rest on each one of us, your children.

Lord, hear us. **Lord, graciously hear us.**

We remember before you the world's joyful diversity and its
desperate needs:

we celebrate those countries where living standards are rising
and freedom is deepening its roots (particularly in . . .);
we celebrate the work of the United Nations as a forum for
peace and justice and the best aspirations of humanity;
we lament the waves of terror affecting every continent, and
the reluctance of governments to address root causes;
we lament the pain of Africa, cut to pieces by the Aids
pandemic, with lives and economies destroyed and orphans
seeking shelter.

May your blessing rest on each nation and its children.

Lord, hear us. **Lord, graciously hear us.**

We remember before you our homes, families and communities:

the relatives and friends to whom we owe so much, and whom
we rarely thank . . . *(short pause)*;
the people we remember with guilt each Christmas – another
year without contact . . . *(short pause)*;
the school nearby where young lives are being shaped and
equipped for life . . . *(short pause)*;
the neighbours who we haven't got to know . . . *(short pause)*;
the local councillors who are trying to build something
better . . . *(short pause)*.

May your blessing rest on each person and place, that your
kingdom may come in them.

Lord, hear us. **Lord, graciously hear us.**

4

We remember before you people in special need, asking for your touch of life:

> on our heart is someone who's ill at home or in hospital . . .
> *(pause)*;
> on our heart is someone deeply lonely and uncertain about
> life . . . *(pause)*;
> on our heart is someone whose own heart is broken . . .
> *(pause)*;
> on our heart is a special life, now lost to us but alive to you . . .
> *(pause)*.

May your blessing rest on each one, for in you is hope, healing and joy.

Lord, hear us. **Lord, graciously hear us.**

Gracious God, we have brought to you the people and the situations we care about most this morning. Be to them more than they dreamed of and more than they dared hope, for we ask it in the name of Jesus, the Giver of Life. Amen.

(2) LET US PRAY 2

*Another straightforward set of intercessions using a standard
shape. Remember that this is only something to start with! Your
own situation may call for many changes in content, and your
own personality may mean many changes in style.*

Heavenly Father and Lord of all Life, we share with you our love
and concern for the world.

We long for peace in . . . .

We ache for the people of . . . .

We share the pain of . . . , facing a new tragedy . . . .

What the television news doesn't tell us is that you are already
working at full stretch in each of these places, and that your
people are in the thick of these difficulties with acts of mercy and
compassion. Help us to remember that where your people are
hurting, you too are wounded; and where your people are
responding in love, you too are in the midst of them.

Lord, hear us. **Lord, graciously hear us.**

We share with you our love and concern for the Church.

We delight in the richness of the Church's spiritual heritage.

We celebrate the stories of faith and the miracles of love among
your people.

We proclaim with serious joy a child's birth, a saviour's death and
a victor's resurrection.

And yet we repent of so much in the Church that dishonours the
gospel – our small-mindedness, our arguments, our negativity.
Show us, Lord, at every level of church life, how to be a
community of the friends of Jesus, blessed by that friendship and

seeking to be a blessing to others. So may your kingdom come afresh in this land.

Lord, hear us. **Lord, graciously hear us.**

We share with you our love and concern for our community and culture.

Thank you for the range of fascinating skills and enthusiasms in each community, especially . . . *(any local project, festival, hobby group in action recently).*

Thank you for the huge hope we have in our children and the efforts we all make to support and encourage them, especially . . . *(events at a local school, children's support agencies, etc.).*

Thank you for those unsung heroes who sustain the fabric of local life, and the voluntary organizations that care for every imaginable need . . . *(any celebrating something special).*

And with our thanks, come our prayers that you will harness all this good will and use it as the raw material for your kingdom.

Lord, hear us. **Lord, graciously hear us.**

We share with you our love and concern for people in a bad place today.

We have on our hearts these people who are ill . . . *(list of the sick).*

We have on our hearts people who are in a tight spot trying to make ends meet . . . *(short pause).*

We have on our hearts people whose relationships have fallen apart . . . *(short pause).*

We have on our hearts people who've been forgotten in prison, on the streets, or in long-term psychiatric care . . . *(short pause).*

Remind us, Father, that every person is as unique and valuable to you as the disciples were to Jesus. Each person is irreplaceable and each your beloved child. Help us to treat each other with the respect and honour we would reserve for you. Please heal the sick, give dignity to the fallen, and draw us all into the fellowship of the redeemed.

Lord, hear us. **Lord, graciously hear us.**

Finally we share with you our love and concern for ourselves, for you commanded us to love our neighbour and ourselves equally. We offer to you our gratitude for so much and our need for so much. In silence now we thank you for particular things . . . *(pause)*. And we ask you for particular things we truly need . . . *(pause)*. Gracious God, please take and use the tentative longings of our hearts.

Lord, hear us. **Lord, graciously hear us.**

We offer these our prayers in hope, in high hope, and in the name of Jesus Christ, our risen Lord. Amen.

(3) LET US PRAY 3

Prayer in public worship has to strike a balance between being sufficiently down-to-earth and sufficiently inclusive. If the subject matter is too particular it will exclude those who don't identify with the experience; if it's too generalized it will fail to engage the congregation. One of the ways of dealing with this problem is to offer a broad category for prayer and then to particularize it. An alternative is to allow people to 'fill in the blanks'. As ever, it's very important to allow enough time for silent prayer and not to panic over the silence! Allowing enough time shows you mean business!

These intercessions will allow plenty of time for our own silent prayer.

Gracious God, it is our privilege to pray for your world and your people, and so we put our prayers at your disposal this day.

We pray for those who are in the news today, whether willingly or not. Especially we pray for . . . *(name particular situations)* . . . *(pause)*.

Lord, hear us. **Lord, graciously hear us.**

We pray for our church community, our life together in Christ, and our witness to the world. Especially we pray for . . . *(any issue, project, event, problem facing the church)* . . . *(pause)*.

Lord, hear us. **Lord, graciously hear us.**

We pray for those who we've met or talked to in the last day or so who have some important issue to face. Especially we pray for dilemmas faced by our own family and friends . . . *(pause)*.
Lord, hear us. **Lord, graciously hear us.**

We pray for those coping with stress at work, at home, or in life generally – feeling the world is a dark and weary place. Especially we pray for any friend or colleague in need now . . . *(pause)*.

Lord, hear us. **Lord, graciously hear us.**

We pray for those who are waiting for something important – a birth, a job, a visit, a hospital appointment, a word of forgiveness. Especially we pray for anyone we know who's longing for love and friendship, and a way out of loneliness . . . *(pause)*.

Lord, hear us. **Lord, graciously hear us.**

We pray for those whose lives are not content, but who have not yet found their home in you. Especially we pray for one or two people we know for whom faith would be a lovely gift . . . *(pause)*.

Lord, hear us. **Lord, graciously hear us.**

Father, every person we have mentioned in our hearts is known and loved by you more than we can ever imagine. We entrust them to you in confidence and hope, knowing that you will use our prayers for their healing and well-being, for we ask these things in the name of Jesus Christ, who is alive forever with you and the Holy Spirit. Amen.

(4) AN ORDINARY SUNDAY

Many Sundays are simply ordinary Sundays – no special name, no special focus. But one of the essential Christian insights is that nothing is ever really ordinary since everything is charged with the glory of God. Our intercessions may contribute to the opening of our doors of perception.

The response to the words 'Lord, in your mercy' is **'hear our prayer'**.

Lord of the Sabbath, for most of us this is an ordinary Sunday, like many before and probably many to come. We're here because we normally come here, not necessarily because we're looking for something, or expecting very much. Take us now in our very ordinariness, and shake us up and pour us out, and make our hearts beat a little faster as we reach out in holy fascination to you . . . *(pause)*.

Lord, in your mercy, **hear our prayer.**

Lord of creation, we admit that sometimes we can miss the glory and the grandeur of your created world. We can walk through life with our senses turned off. Give us, we pray, the gift of caring contemplation, so that we may see all things shot through with your glory: the morning sun between the houses, the endless shades of darkness in an evening sky, the image of Christ in the face of a friend. And sometimes, let us see things that are so beautiful they almost make us afraid . . . *(pause)*.

Lord, in your mercy, **hear our prayer.**

Lord of the nations, we know that peace doesn't seem likely in . . . . But in this world surprises constantly catch us out. The surprise of an entire political system collapsing before the freedom of the human spirit. The surprise of captives emerging from kidnap with

their lives and hopes intact. The surprise of forgiveness, and a man who lays down his gun. So, Lord, we *do* dare to pray – bring peace in . . . and base that peace on justice . . . *(pause)*.
Lord, in your mercy, **hear our prayer.**

Lord of our shared lives, we live too much for ourselves, islands of self-sufficiency in an ocean of needs; we fail to help the needy; and we fail to receive their gifts. We fail to see beyond our own little world. Help us to venture out, to encounter others in their struggles and in their generosity. We bring to you now both someone we know who's struggling, and someone we know who's celebrating. Help us to be aware of them, and help them to be aware of you . . . *(pause)*.

Lord, in your mercy **hear our prayer.**

Lord of the ordinary, give us eyes to see the deep mystery of ordinary things, ears to hear your quiet thunder, hearts to stir to the promise of resurrection. So transform our week ahead that we may constantly glimpse your glory and respond with joy. Reveal to us the extraordinary depths of every ordinary moment, and in that moment, transfigure us . . . *(pause)*.

Lord, in your mercy, **hear our prayer.**

(5) A SUMMER SUNDAY

Worship on summer Sundays often goes on without any sense of high drama. These are occasions to change the mood of our intercessions to try and match the mood of the season. The following intercessions are much improved if local colour can be added at appropriate points.

A summer Sunday, and lots of people are just getting up, having a lazy breakfast, getting ready for a day in the garden. Sunday papers, lunch at the pub. And most of them don't even think of coming to church. Lord, we can't have made you very attractive to them, or shown the kind of quality of life which would have made them interested to know more. In silence now we think of one person or one family who we know, who we would love to find faith in you. We pray that they might want to know more . . . *(pause).*

Lord, in your mercy, **hear our prayer.**

Some of our own church family are on holiday this week. Benidorm or Bognor, the Lakes or Lanzarote – wherever it is, Father we pray for them now. We hold in our mind's eye and before you, someone or some couple or family who we know, who are away on holiday. And we pray that you'll refresh them deep down inside. Give them time to catch up with themselves, space to get life in perspective again, and the stimulus of new things around them. We pray for them now . . . *(pause).*

Lord, in your mercy, **hear our prayer.**

Even in the media it sometimes seems that a summer Sunday is a time when news stops happening. Silly stories fill the pages. But deep down we know that quiet suffering still goes on. That lady we sometimes meet still has terminal cancer; that new mother is still barely coping with post-natal depression; that man is still

13

putting in five job applications a week, and 30,000 children still die *every day* around the world from hunger and disease. Lord, keep us praying for those who still suffer . . . *(pause)*.

Lord, in your mercy, **hear our prayer.**

Lord, we bring to you our thoughts and prayers this summer Sunday. It's good to be alive; it's good to have this rhythm of life – Sunday rest, summer break. It's good to be here, bringing everything back to you in this (Communion) service, every ordinary part of our lives, every ordinary gift we receive from your hands. Take us and bless us, we pray, and change our ordinary time into your extraordinary time. And in the silence, Lord, we bring our particular needs to you for this coming week . . . *(pause)*.

Lord, in your mercy, **hear our prayer.**
And bless this summer Sunday. **Amen.**

(6) A WINTER SUNDAY

Not every Sunday feels special, even though every Sunday is a
reminder of the resurrection! Sometimes the Church's year just
keeps on turning and we need to pray in the ordinariness of a
winter Sunday. But in the economy of God, nothing is 'just'
ordinary – everything is capable of greater or smaller
transformation. That's the reminder implicit in this prayer.

Gracious God, we've come to you again this day in a place we
love and with people we care for. This winter Sunday doesn't feel
all that special but we thank you for it anyway, and for the
familiarity of this place of prayer where so much is celebrated
throughout the year. Thank you for the stones *(bricks?)*, the
wood, the decoration, the architecture of this place where we
bring our joys and sorrows week by week. And thank you for the
'living stones' – the people with whom we share this place.

Lord, hear us. **Lord, graciously hear us.**

Winter weather has us in its grip, and we try hard to keep warm
and to minimize the discomfort. We pray for those who are
especially vulnerable in cold weather, the elderly, the housebound
and the sick. We pray for some who are known to us, and for
many who are not known to us . . . *(pause)*. And in particular we
pray that everyone in our community will be good neighbours,
alert and thoughtful, and actively aware of vulnerable people
around us.

Lord, hear us. **Lord, graciously hear us.**

Winter has its own compensations – evenings in, hot drinks,
football on the television, the pleasure of warming up, the joy of a
snug home. Give us, Father, quiet pleasure in simple things, so that
out of the ordinary experiences of life we may have a growing
confidence in your kindly presence in every place and at every

time. We pray for those who especially need that assurance at the moment, the 'knowledge within knowledge' that you are present, and in your presence is comfort, hope and peace. So we name in our hearts some people in particular need of that assurance – people who are ill, or anxious, or lonely, or afraid . . . *(pause)*.

Lord, hear us. **Lord, graciously hear us.**

Winter is a time of looking back and looking forward. We look back with thankfulness to the warm summer days, the garden, the holidays, even the threats of water shortage! But we also look forward to the first stirrings of nature, the lengthening days, the first time the sun feels warm again, the sight of snowdrops and daffodils. In the meantime, Creator God of every season of the year, enable us to wait patiently and enjoy the particular gifts of every time and season. Keep us present to each present moment.

Lord, hear us. **Lord, graciously hear us.**

Gracious God of every season and every mood,
in spring we shall know your faithfulness,
in summer we shall know your abundance,
in autumn we shall know your completeness,
in winter we shall know your rest,
and all in the blessed company of Jesus Christ our Lord.

(7) SEASONS OF THE SPIRIT

Images from the natural world evoke a response in most of us. It can be helpful therefore to use one of nature's patterns as the pattern of our prayer. The seasons of the year are full of resonances which make them especially useful as a vehicle for our intercessions. But we need to beware of sentimentality!

The response to the words 'Lord, the seasons change' is **'but your love lasts for ever'**.

Spring is the time of new growth stirring in the heart of nature, when creation wakes and puts out feelers towards the sun and all of life seems to be a glorious possibility. We see this same springtime in the lives of our children, excitedly exploring the possibilities of their lives and their environment. And we see that same springtime in the innovation and imagination of the human spirit as a new business is started up, a new marriage is formed, a new personal challenge is taken on. So, Father, we ask your blessing on us and on our children, thinking particularly of children in our family or in our church, or children we know whose springtime is delayed by illness or disability . . . (*pause*). And we ask your blessing on those we know who are taking new risks in their jobs or their commitments or their dreams, people we name silently now . . . (*pause*).

Lord, the seasons change, **but your love lasts for ever.**

Summer is the time of fullness, when nature luxuriates in its achievements. Summer assaults the senses with the smell of freshly cut grass, birdsong in the morning, the long shadows at the end of a golden day. We too have periods when life is full and everything is good and nothing seems impossible. Lord, we thank you for those times – times past, times present, or times still to hope for. We thank you also for those times, good and full, enjoyed by members of our family, or church family. Help us always to see life as a gift. May we always pray: 'For what we have received, may the Lord make us truly thankful.'

Lord, the seasons change, **but your love lasts for ever.**

Autumn comes upon us as a gradual closing down. A final exuberant burst of colour, swirling leaves, evening chill, nature settling down to sleep. The mood of autumn is reflective, pondering the turning of the years. So we too, sometimes, have autumn in our hearts as we adjust to a gentler stage of life, perhaps facing advancing years, or some debilitation or loss. There is beauty in this time as memory and experience combine to give wisdom and a deeper grasp of what's important. But some people are full of melancholy and sadness. So we picture some people now, entering their autumn with gratitude or with a sense of loss, and we pray for them quietly in our hearts . . . (*pause*).

Lord, the seasons change, **but your love lasts for ever.**

Winter is the time of rest, of darkness and of short, sharp days. It's the time of keeping warm and hopeful as the deep engines of nature tick over quietly, awaiting their call to recreate the earth. We too get on with life as best we can in these dark days, preparing for that burst of light on December the 25th and planning our holidays in that far-off land of sun, sand and sea. But there are many who normally experience life as winter – a time of dark struggle, with illness, with poverty, with cruel relationships, with the daily wounds of injustice. For them there is little of winter's comfort, its rest and the joy of Christmas. There are some we know for whom life is perpetual winter. There are countless others whom we don't know, especially in . . . (*places of poverty, war and oppression*). We pray for them, and that you, Lord, may find ways to lighten their darkness.

Lord, the seasons change, **but your love lasts for ever.**

Lord of the seasons, carry us through our years with hearts and minds open to see and receive all that you have to give, so that we may experience the gracious cycle of your love and mercy, which we have known supremely in Jesus Christ our Lord.

(8) FAMILY

One of our most significant experiences in life is that of 'family'. There's no better – or worse – context for bringing up children. There's no greater delight – or wounding – than being an adult in a family. But the category has other applications too, in the family of the Church, for example, or the family of nations. Here, then, is a rich seam to explore in intercession because everyone understands the importance of the concept. We have to be aware, of course, that the concept has this very double-edged potential, and we must therefore weigh our words carefully.

The response to the words 'We bow our knees before the Father' is '**from whom every family takes its name**'.

Father, we have come from you and we take our life from your hand. You have placed us in families, not of our choosing, but of your giving. You have entrusted us to each other. As we think now of the families that nurtured us we pause to give thanks; or to grieve; or to be angry; at the least to *recognize* that we have been shaped by our families . . . *(pause)*. Some of us no longer have many family members, but we give thanks for those who have become surrogate families to us, sharing and blessing our lives with warmth and love. We remember and pray now for some of our family for whom we have a special care and responsibility, or who are going through especially testing times at the moment . . . *(pause)*.

We bow our knees before the Father, **from whom every family takes its name.**

One description of the Church is 'the family of God'. Lord, you see us in the Church loving and squabbling, fighting and forgiving, and living out all the dynamics of human family life. We take this as both a privilege and a problem and ask you to inhabit our life together so fully that hostility is squeezed out. Be our vision, our strength, our companion, so that we never try to take back the life of your Church and claim it as our own. In silence now we hand over to you any particular issues facing us as your church family together – plans, problems, people in need, whatever is on our heart . . . *(pause)*.

We bow our knees before the Father, **from whom every family takes its name.**

We sometimes wistfully speak of the family of nations, expressing our belief that this is how it should be. But we know that family matters at this level often become very bitter and violent in different parts of the world. In particular we carry in our hearts the painful experiences of . . . and . . . *(terrorism, violence, rumours of war in the news)*. We pray, Father, for your peaceful Spirit to permeate the hearts and minds of the leaders of the nations, the elders of the family, on whom so much rests. Particularly we pray for you to give your servants . . . the gift of . . . .

We bow our knees before the Father, **from whom every family takes its name.**

Father, what we have prayed for, answer. What we should have prayed for, remember. What we regret, forgive. And what we are, bless. For Jesus' sake.

(9) KEEP THE PEACE

Intercessions often benefit from focusing on one important theme which runs through the whole, rather than four or five diverse themes which try to cover everything we can think of! The theme of peace is one which concerns us all. As ever, current events and local concerns should give specific content to the prayers.

The response to the words 'Blessed are the peacemakers' is **'for they will be called children of God'**.

Lord, in a world of violence we ask you to do so much. Our hands are tied without you and, amazingly, your hands are tied without us. So we ask you today to keep the peace and carry the load, and show us how to do that too.

Blessed are the peacemakers, **for they will be called children of God.**

Martin Luther King said we had a choice: a world at peace or a world in pieces. As we look at a world map we can see the fires of war in many places – sometimes threatening, as in . . . , sometimes smouldering, as in . . . , sometimes well alight, as in . . . . Violence and warfare seem to act like a forest fire, breaking out in different places in the heat of our hatreds, jealousies and tribalism. Lord, permeate our lives with the desire for peace. Wherever there's a chink of opportunity, let your peaceable Spirit enter the hearts of leaders and warlords of every creed and colour. Bring us to our senses; bring us to our knees, and bring us back to you.

Blessed are the peacemakers, **for they will be called children of God.**

Lord, we look for peace closer to home, in our own communities and indeed our own churches. Our communities are still threatened by our personal prejudices based on race, class and political beliefs. Our churches are still undermined by the arrogance of the self-righteous and by our inability to love one another. In silence we call to mind and hold before you some of these places in society and in the Church where we are failing to keep to the ways of peace . . . *(pause)*. Lord, work on us with the alchemy of your Spirit so that we grow into the mind and character of Christ.

Blessed are the peacemakers, **for they will be called children of God.**

Lord, often our violence is rooted in our inner conflicts and our unfinished attempts to grow up. Where once we fought in the school playground, now we fight in our marriages and offices and committees. By your Spirit help us to grow in grace so that we can put things in perspective, step back from the brink of conflict, and speak your words of peace. In silence, we each call to mind an area of conflict in which we have some involvement or where we could be a peacemaker, and we ask for the wisdom and strength of your Spirit to be an agent of peace in that place . . . *(pause)*.

Blessed are the peacemakers, **for they will be called children of God.**

Lord, we stand amidst the wreckage of a world too often at war, communities too often in dispute, and lives too often in despair. But we hold to the vision that you will wipe away every tear from our eyes, and death will be no more; and mourning and crying and pain will be no more, for the first things – the things of war – will have passed away.

Until then, O God, we ask you to keep the peace and carry the load, and show us how to do that too, so that finally we may be called children of God who followed the Son – Jesus Christ our Lord.

(10) MUSIC

Music plays a very important part in our spiritual journeying. For one thing, hymns are often more remembered than biblical texts. New Christian songs have been the vehicle for much renewal in the life of the Church. And great music always has the capacity to touch people profoundly. If our spirituality is so deeply shaped by music it follows that it can be helpful sometimes to make music the basis of our prayer, either by praying about it or by using it (see The Intercessions Handbook, *pp. 98–103). Here is a way of praying about music as a major factor in our Christian pilgrimage.*

The response to the words 'O sing to the Lord a new song' is **'sing his praise in the congregation'** (Psalm 149).

Lord of beauty and harmony, who gave us music for joy and celebration, for sadness and consolation, and for faith and inspiration – thank you for the wealth of music we have available to us in worship. Thank you for great hymnwriters of old – Charles Wesley, Isaac Watts, George Herbert and others – and for their modern counterparts, all seeking to take our hearts and minds to heavenly places. Help us to invest our faith more fully in our singing, so that, when we sing, we think about the words, and the One to whom we are singing.

O sing to the Lord a new song, **sing his praise in the congregation.**

Lord of beauty and harmony, of cadence and interval, who puts music in our hearts and a longing for perfection, thank you for the capacity of great music to move and inspire us, and to disturb and question us. May we give ourselves fully to that experience as one of the many routes you offer to the joy of your presence. May those for whom faith is difficult, find in music a voice they recognize and discover it to be yours. And may the musicians we listen to so carefully, honour the composer's art, the listener's response, and the Lord of all creativity as they give life to the music before them.

O sing to the Lord a new song, **sing his praise in the congregation.**

Lord of beauty and harmony, thank you for those who lead the praises of your people, the choirs and organists, the music groups and soloists. We pray for those who lead our music in this place, asking in silence now for your richest blessing on them and on what they offer . . . In particular, we pray for . . . *(specific need in music resources, an upcoming service, choice of new hymnbook, etc.)*. And we pray that our music may increasingly fill our hearts with a desire and love for you.

O sing to the Lord a new song, **sing his praise in the congregation.**

Lord of beauty and harmony, we confess that our lives often fail to reflect the harmony of your peace. In silence we lament the discord of our lives and the conflicts in our community . . . May our hearts grow ever more responsive to the melody of your love moving deeply through our lives. So give us the desire to live our days closer to you – the One who composed our lives with such originality and patience.

O sing to the Lord a new song, **sing his praise in the congregation.**

Let all the world, in every corner sing – my God and King!

(11) TASTE

Increasingly, Christian people are finding that the use of the senses is a rich way into prayer. We need to resist the reduction of public prayer to a diet of 'touchy-feely' meanderings, so a certain rigour is required. But the appeal of the five senses through which we all experience the world is an obvious route for the intercessor to explore. Here is just one of those senses.

The response to the words 'Taste and see' is **'that the Lord is good'**.

Gracious God, you enrich our lives with an abundance of good things and our tables overflow with your generosity. We relish the huge range of tastes available to us on the supermarket shelves. Taste upon taste, gift upon gift. Make us truly thankful for every meal and for the abundant earth which pours forth this astonishing harvest.

Taste and see **that the Lord is good.**

Gracious God, you call us all to your table, to share the tastes of eternal life, both now and hereafter. Enable us to open our homes to each other and to share the gifts of field and farm, of warmth and friendship, through the hospitality to which you call us. We pray that the way we welcome each other may reflect the way you welcome us into your kingdom.

Taste and see **that the Lord is good.**

Gracious God, we recognize that the abundance of our supermarkets is not shared by huge numbers of your children around the world. They can't taste what they haven't got. We pray for a realignment of the world's trade relationships, that justice may be done for every developing nation. Strengthen the trade justice movement, and move the minds of the rich to embrace the needs of the poor. Especially we pray at the moment for . . . *(the latest actions, conferences, negotiations, famine or drought)*.

May we *all* taste and see **that the Lord is good.**

Gracious God, most of us experience life as a feast of opportunities. Each day has a host of things to do, of people to meet and interests to pursue. But there are others around us who experience their days as lonely and bleak, without close friends or work or money or health. Each of us knows a number of people who find life at present far from the rich feast you intend. We name them in our hearts now, and pray that they may know your sustaining presence, a change in their circumstances, and a taste of good things . . . *(pause)*.

May they taste and see **that the Lord is good.**

Many people find it hard to taste that God is good, or indeed to taste God at all. Father, we pray that we may find ways to offer the taste of your goodness to our family, friends and others in our community. In silence we pray for one or two particular people who we wish could taste your goodness . . . *(pause)*. And if we're honest, there are times when most of us Christians lose the taste of the divine as well. *So* when *we're* struggling, we pray that you will find ways to draw us back to the wonderful tastes of your table.

Taste and see **that the Lord is good.**

As we gather together at the table of the Lord, we anticipate the feast at the end of the world. Thank you for that glimpse of all your people reconciled to each other and to you in a glorious banquet. In the meantime, may the taste of bread and wine keep us pressing on and working for that day when all God's people say to each other:

Taste and see **that the Lord is good.** (Bring it on Lord; bring it on!)

(12) WATER OF LIFE

Nothing is more integral to life than water. Few things destroy life more quickly than the absence of water, and unclean water is the biggest cause of child mortality in developing countries. Conversely, when water appears in the desert it makes the thirsty land blossom immediately. Jesus used water as one of his most powerful images for the life he came to offer. We can use the image ourselves in a number of ways. Here is one.

Jesus promised the woman at the well that he could give her living water which would well up inside her forever.

The response to the words 'Lord of living water' is '**quench our thirst, we pray**'.

Lord, we delight in the gift of water, which we drink to stay alive, and in which we shower to stay clean. We love to be refreshed by it on a baking hot day and to splash and swim in it on a well-earned holiday. Water cleanses us both outside and in; it runs through our lives as a sign of hope. In so many ways, water is holy. Let us never take water for granted.

Lord of living water, **quench our thirst, we pray.**

Water gives us life, but to many it brings death. We know that water-borne diseases kill millions of children every year in the Two-Thirds World. No taps to turn; no filters to clear the water; no sewers but the one into the river. Forgive us, Lord, for abusing such a gift. Help your greedy world – and that means 'us' with our comfortable lifestyle – to make clean water, deep wells and basic hygiene one of our main priorities for development aid.

Lord of living water, **quench our thirst, we pray.**

Lord, how have we managed to make even water a weapon of war? In the Middle East water is a political issue; in the West terrorists want to poison it. We pray for those who misuse the gifts of creation so badly. May they recognize the holiness of water and the sanctity of life. And may our longing for justice be used to cleanse and heal the world. (*Especially we pray for . . . .*)

Lord of living water, **quench our thirst, we pray.**

Best of all, you promise us living water, bubbling up within us as a source of irrepressible hope and joy. Help us in our daily lives to be inwardly still so that we can be aware of your graceful activity within us. And help us to be generous in sharing the living water of the gospel in what we say and do. We pray in silence for some of the people and the places where that gift of life and hope may be needed . . . .

Lord of living water, **quench our thirst, we pray.**
And because we drink this water, may we never be thirsty again.

(13) COLOURS OF THE RAINBOW

*We're surrounded by a constant kaleidoscope of colour, and we're
more affected by it than we might realize. (Designers and artists
are well aware of its power!) We can harness the deep
connections made by colour in various forms of intercession, and
we can do it even more effectively if we can demonstrate those
colours, for example with coloured gels on an overhead
projector. Be imaginative!*

To the words 'Lord of the rainbow', please respond '**hear our
prayer**'.

Lord, after the Flood you put your rainbow in the skies to remind
us of the promises you made to your people. Now we claim those
promises as we pray to you.

Lord of the rainbow, **hear our prayer.**

Green – the colour of creation. There's so much green, Lord, and
so much beauty in our world. Help us to stop, look and listen to
your creation – the amazing world of plants and the canopy of
trees, the peace of green fields and the thunder of the seas. And
yet daily we're destroying your world and abusing our privilege
as stewards of creation. May we turn again, and love, honour and
conserve what you have so graciously given.

Lord of the rainbow, **hear our prayer.**

Yellow – the colour of the sun, of warmth and light, and so the
colour of smiles and love and friendship. Thank you, Father, for
the delight we have in family, friends and special communities.
Thank you in particular for our special people who we think of
quietly now . . . . We pray for those who have few friends, whose
loneliness is a daily burden, and for those who seem unable to
make or keep the friendships that are so life-giving to others.

Lord of the rainbow, **hear our prayer.**

Red – the colour of blood, the blood of the martyrs and saints who gave their lives for the faith we often hold so lightly. We pray for the Church that nurtured both them and us. Give to your Church in every culture and nation, the courage to be different, to speak the truth and live the life that draws others to Jesus Christ. Especially we pray for this church and our neighbouring churches, that we may be beacons of light in this community. *(Particular needs can be mentioned.)*

Lord of the rainbow, **hear our prayer.**

Blue – the colour of the United Nations' flag. Today that blue flag is having to fly in very many places because so often people opt for ways of hatred, violence, rape and robbery, when you've given our world more than enough for all to prosper. Have mercy on us, and strengthen the desire of all people to live their lives in friendship, cooperation and mutual care, against a backdrop of justice and honest peace. Especially we pray for . . . .

Lord of the rainbow, **hear our prayer.**

Green for creation and yellow for warm relationships; red for the blood of the martyrs and blue for the flag of the UN. And there's orange for the sweet fruits of the earth, and indigo for the colour of shadows, and violet for the colour of sorrow. Lord God, you surround us with so much colour, and the colours of the rainbow combine in the white light of your dazzling presence. So, take the prayers we've offered, together with the promises you've given us, and bring all creation to the fulfilment of your kingdom, where prayers and promises are no more, for Christ is all in all.

Lord of the rainbow, **hear our prayer.**

31

(14) CIRCLES OF PRAYER

There seems to be something deeply satisfying in this way of prayer. People respond to the image of a stone being dropped in a pond and creating circles that ripple gently outwards. The content of the 'ripples' can be as varied as our imagination.

Imagine for a moment that our prayers are like circles in a pond made by throwing a stone into the water. The smooth surface of the pond is broken as the stone drops in, and we see the first circle emerge.

In this circle are the people with us here *(in church)* right now. Around us are members of the family of God, people we know well or with whom we've shared many Easters. These are our special brothers and sisters on the road to God. We need each other. Let's then pray for the people alongside us now, those beside us, around us, in front of us, wherever. Silently, let's pray for each other's well-being, as fully as we know how . . . .

Silence

The circle spreads. Look now at the second circle. Here are the people living around *this church* in the wider community. Our cities and towns depend on the teachers, the local politicians, the postal workers, the checkout staff at the supermarkets. We would be so much the poorer without the charity workers, the bank clerks, the gardeners in the park. These are people we see but don't often register, let alone pray for. Who stands out for each of us in this second circle, now we think of it? Who needs our prayer, now? And what might they need from a God who wants to give them everything? . . .

Silence

The circle spreads again. Look now at the third circle. People with a national profile, the people we see on television, political leaders, sports people, celebrities, criminals, people who are famous for a day (though maybe hurt for a lifetime). These are often people under colossal pressure. Who have we seen like that recently – perhaps on TV? So many to pray for. So let us each choose one or two people, and hold them up to the embrace and the mercy of God, who has so much to give . . . .

Silence

The circles spread right out. They reach the far edges of the pond; one after another they lap against the banks. Out here is the struggle of our whole creation to live up to God's glorious purposes. This is where prayer, science, poetry and politics all meet. For this is where God's will is done (or not), his kingdom comes (or not), on earth as it is in heaven. Here God is constantly urging his world into freedom and wholeness. Let us gladly align ourselves with him as he serves and saves his world . . . .

Silence

Lord God our Father, our prayer this day is only a stone thrown into a pool, a tiny offering of love in an ocean of need. Please take our prayers, along with the prayers of millions of others, and bring about your purposes of love, healing and hope to the very edges of the world. Through Jesus Christ our Lord.

33

(15) DAY-TO-DAY WORLD

One of the perennial problems with intercessions in public worship is that they tend to float several feet off the ground. Congregations can hardly be blamed for failing to engage with such prayers when they simply don't come down to the earthly experiences that are the stuff of their ordinary lives. What follows is one attempt to make the connections.

Dear Lord and Father of all humanity, we bring our prayers to you not just for this special day but for everyday, the everyday world in which we try to follow you from dawn to dusk, and often lose our way. But in this day-to-day world we depend utterly on so many people you give us. In our prayers we celebrate them, thank you for them, and pray for their well-being.

The response to the words 'Bless our day-to-day world' is '**Bless our day-to-day people**'.

When we get up in the morning we depend on workers in the water industry to supply us with water for the shower, power workers who enable us to turn on the light and the kettle, radio broadcasters who give us instant information about the day's news, and so many others. Thank you Father for each one – for their skill, judgement and willingness to get up early!

Bless our day-to-day world. **Bless our day-to-day people.**

As the day gets under way, we depend on transport workers who run train and bus services and maintain our road system; we depend on shop workers who provide for our necessities and our whims; we depend on gardeners who keep our parks and flower beds beautiful, and street cleaners to keep our streets usable; we depend on IT maintenance teams to keep our computers running. Thank you Father for each one – for their contribution to the complex web of support that keeps us all on the road.

Bless our day-to-day world. **Bless our day-to-day people.**

As the day wears on, we depend on the long chain of supply that brings coffee from South America to our kitchen or our desk; we depend on telephone engineers who keep us in touch with everybody else; we depend on the underpaid people who run sandwich shops and eating places; we depend (let's face it) on sewage workers who perform a vital task. Thank you Father for this army of people who enable us to get on with what we have to do.

Bless our day-to-day world. **Bless our day-to-day people.**

We come towards the evening. We've depended on teachers to equip our children for life, medical staff to be ready for our illnesses and accidents, writers who've prepared the scripts for the evening's TV, cleaners who now go through our offices. So many people; so much we take for granted. Thank you Father for the gifts we all bring to the engines of our society and the health of our nation.

Bless our day-to-day world. **Bless our day-to-day people.**

And bless, Lord, also, those who now stand and wait, those who stay at home, their working days at an end. Enable them to value the dignity of rest, the wisdom of experience and the possibilities of the Third Age. For all of us are in your hands and the web of life is incomplete without any of us.

So Lord, bless your world; bless it with thankfulness and fulfilment, bless it with kindness and hope, and bring it finally to completion in Jesus Christ our Lord.

(16) PARTICULAR PEOPLE

The method here is that of painting pictures of situations of need through the 'window' of particular (fictitious) people. The situations can come from any places in the news or in relief agency literature. The people are imaginary portraits, so the actual prayer is for 'people like' the person named.

Today we're going to pray for those living in need and poverty, and we're going to do it by using brief word-pictures of individual people, remembering that it's people, not statistics, who are hungry and in need.

Chandri is 31 years old. He lives in a corrugated iron shack on the edge of the city. He picks up work when he can. He lost his wife and child through cholera, but he wants to start again. He loves life, music, children, even the odd game of cricket when there's space and a ball. He has no money, and only a few possessions, but he wants to love someone, build a new family, make plans for a better future.

So let's pray now in silence for people like Chandri all over the world, people in need of love and hope . . . *(pause).*

Olga is 18. She's optimistic and cheerful, but then you need that in Russia these days. She's a student, reading English, and good at it. Mother is divorced, money hard to come by. A loaf of bread costs 300 times more today than it did a few years ago. How do you keep up with that? It's hard to know what will happen politically; it's all very fragile. But this is Olga's country, Holy Russia, and she wants to see it through. At least the churches are opening again, and the icons are sparkling in the candle-light, and the priests are adjusting to all the new demands. Olga drops into church most days, and then she feels stronger.

So let's pray now in silence for people like Olga, people in need of stability and determination . . . *(pause)*.

Jim used to have a job. A flat and a family too. But the factory closed; his job with it. He lost his confidence and couldn't find work. So then the days were long, lunchtime TV and afternoon TV, lunchtime drink and afternoon drink. Rows at home, more rows, and him leaving. London without a job or money isn't much fun. Nor is Waterloo Bridge, and a cardboard mattress. Does Jim have a future or just a long past?

So let's pray in silence for people like Jim, people in need of a break and a new start . . . (pause).

Lord Jesus, you came with love from your heavenly Father, and still today you come with love for every human being, the ones we know and love ourselves, and also the ones we pass in the bus queue, see on the news or know only as statistics. Lord, revive our imagination so that we see you in every human life. Revive our capacity to love, so that we serve you gladly wherever you make yourself known to us. So we shall truly be agents of your kingdom of hope and love, here on earth. Amen.

(17) THE GLOBAL CHURCH

One of the temptations of church life is to become preoccupied with local concerns and to forget the vast family of which we are a part. These intercessions start with the local but move into the global. Particular international links and partnerships can be inserted as appropriate, as can trouble spots or places in the news.

Companions in Christ, let us pray for the Church and for the churches, and rejoice with our neighbours around the world, held with us in the embrace of God's love.

Lord, hear us as we pray for the churches of other denominations in our neighbourhood, particularly . . . and . . . . May they prosper in every way; may people come to faith there, and may their witness in the community be clear and attractive. We pray for our relationships with them as part of the one great Church for which Jesus prayed. Bring to our hearts a real desire to think and plan as churches together, particularly over . . . *(local opportunity).*

Lord, hear us. **Lord, graciously hear us.**

Lord, hear us as we pray for a bigger vision in our church life. Take us out of our small world of local Christian activities. Place us on the map of your worldwide Church, where white Christians are far outnumbered by those of other colours, and the churches of Africa and the Pacific rim are growing momentously. Father, we pray for these new churches, for maturity and resources to cope with their numbers. May we be willing and eager to receive the gifts they can offer us. Particularly we pray for . . . *(local church link with the church overseas).*

Lord, hear us. **Lord, graciously hear us.**

Lord, hear us as we pray for the parts of your Church which are suffering today. In recent years we've heard of Christians stoned in Asia, crucified in Africa, tortured in Central America, and assassinated in Eastern Europe. When faith and evil clash, the stakes are high. Lord, make our spirits restless for justice, and our prayers serious for freedom; and never let us forget our brothers and sisters in pain . . . *(pause)*.

Lord, hear us. **Lord, graciously hear us.**

Lord, hear us as we pray for the future role of the global Church. May we recognize the need for one united witness to a world which plays daily with the vicious toys of death, and is deeply corrupted by its desire for power and wealth. May the Church be a joyful alternative to these values; may we speak fearlessly but tenderly to the world for which Christ died. We pray now that the Church may be one, alive in Christ and committed to the world's needs . . . *(pause)*.

Lord, hear us. **Lord, graciously hear us.**

Lord of the Church, hear us as we look to you for vision and energy in these testing days. Renew your Church throughout the world – and start with us. Amen

(18) O GOD, WHY?

We're most stretched in our intercessions when some terrible tragedy has occurred and it's hard to know how to pray without sounding banal. Perhaps the most important need is to be honest; hence the response in this intercession, 'O God, why?' Public intercession isn't the time for theological reasoning; it's more a time for honest emotion before God. We shouldn't try to tidy up tragedy in neat prayers. Perhaps questioning and impotence is the most effective way of identifying with the depth of sorrow felt by so many.

To the words 'And so we say', please feel free to reply '**O God, why?**'

Lord, we've seen the pictures, and felt the shock, of . . . . It seems so tragic, so pointless, so desperate. We've heard the stories, the little cameos of grief, and we feel so helpless. Sometimes we rage against this kind of event, and sometimes we feel a sense of dull fatalism that 'this is the way the world is'.

And so we say, **O God, why?**

In the meantime our prayers seem futile, like stones in our mouths. Words of any kind seem trivial and clumsy. How can we pray in these situations? How can we frame anything worth saying? How did Mary pray at the crucifixion?

And so we say, **O God, why?**

We believe you're somehow there in the mess of it all. At least that's what our faith tells us. But just at the moment that doesn't feel to be enough. We know you're helping the helpless, as well as helping the helpers, but the point is – it all seems too late.

And so we say, **O God, why?**

We'll do our best to clear up the mess, and we'll move on. But there are many who won't be able to move on because they'll have been too much changed by this event, and too traumatized. We know you'll stay with them every step of the way, and you'll be at full stretch to bring them healing . . . .

But still we say, **O God, why?**

All we can do is light a candle in the darkness, which now we do *(light a large candle)*. It represents our fragile prayer and our battered faith. And as it burns, let it be for us a sign of your love and grace, shining in our present darkness. We'll keep now a time of silence for sorrow and reflection and aching before God . . . *(a longer than usual pause)*.

Make us *im*patient for that day when the whole creation shall be renewed and we have a new heaven and a new earth,

and we shall no longer say, 'O God, why?'

Amen, Lord, so be it.

(19) THE STREAM

The idea of progression is very helpful in giving prayer a sense of direction and purpose. There are many ways of doing this and others will be seen throughout this book, but here is one which takes the familiar image of the stream as it bounces downhill. The initial painting of the picture mustn't be rushed because people have to 'own' the picture they are being offered before they can use it.

Think for a moment of a stream bouncing down the mountainside, clear, fresh, and playful. It sparkles in the sun. Nothing can hold back its enthusiasm. Let that be a picture of how we feel about the good and joyful things in our life – the people, the events, the daily miracles of nature, the details of seeing and breathing and touching. Let's remember when our spirits rose this week, when life felt pure and true. As the stream enjoys its very nature, let's enjoy the memory of those good things – and in silence, be thankful . . . *(pause)*.

The stream bounces on, full of itself, full of potential, but inevitably it runs into obstacles – boulders and fallen branches and the accumulation of debris. We too run into obstacles that fall across our path, debris from our mistakes, boulders that seem too hard to shift. So we name those obstacles now, being honest with our hearts . . . *(pause)*. But we also watch the stream. It may not be able to force its way through the problems, but it's endlessly inventive in finding another way – around, or beneath, or above. The love of God is inexhaustible and irresistible. Let's see that love carrying us over or under or around whatever obstacles are set before us today . . . *(pause)*.

The stream is bolder now, fuller, more sure of itself. It's joined by other streams that have made their own journeys and brought their own character as a gift to others. Who has God given each of us as a gift? Who brings grace into our life? Who has brought us the greatest gift of all – the love of God in a form we can understand? We give thanks for these people who have come into our lives, and pray for them, that they may continue to radiate the presence of Christ . . . *(pause)*.

Now the stream has become a river, growing all the time. There are people in the water, struggling against it, clinging to the wreckage of their hopes, waving for help. We know many people who today feel swept away by difficulties too great for them to manage. Let's name them in our hearts and pray for them with conviction. For the Lord will lift them up, and enable them to float safely in the high tide of his love. So we pray for them now . . . *(pause)*.

Now the river is broad, mighty and unstoppable, surging to the sea. We're caught up in the power and the purpose of the river. Who can imagine it started as a tiny stream, bubbling over the high slopes? The ways of God are huge in scale and irresistible in purpose. He seeks to renew the face of the earth, and we are part of the plan – the river, the people of God. So we savour the certain knowledge that the earth shall be filled with the glory of God, as the waters cover the sea . . . *(pause)*.

Lord of boundless energy, you refuse to be beaten; always you reinvent yourself to achieve the impossible. Give us such confidence in your life running through us and through the world, that nothing will stop you achieving your joyous purposes of love, life, hope and justice. This we ask in the name of Jesus Christ our Lord. Amen.

(20) FREEDOM

The cry for freedom is universal. We hear it from ethnic groups, political minorities, subjugated peoples, oppressed women – and teenagers everywhere! It has a ready echo in our hearts and a deep resonance in the gospel where the promise is that, 'if the Son shall set us free, we shall be free indeed'. This makes the theme of freedom a strong one to work with in intercession. Topical situations are, as ever, a vital ingredient.

The response to the words 'If the Son shall set us free' is '**we shall be free indeed**'.

Life-giving God, one of your most characteristic actions is to set people free. As you freed your people from Egypt, from Babylon, and finally – on the Cross – from everything that would destroy us, so we ask you to set your Church free in this age from the divisions, rivalries and obsessions that put us back in chains. So we ask you to save us from ourselves in our arguments over . . . (*e.g. women bishops, human sexuality, church unity, money*). Give us the deep security that enables us to give each other freedom to be different.

If the Son shall set us free, **we shall be free indeed.**

Life-giving God, one of your most characteristic actions is to give people hope. There's a wonderful roll-call of those who, with invincible hope, have fought for freedom without using violence – Wilberforce, Bonhoeffer, Gandhi, Martin Luther King, many peoples in eastern Europe. But still the people of your world suffer the terrible imprisonments of political systems, debt, hunger, torture, Aids and so much more. We pray earnestly for people imprisoned by . . . in . . . and by . . . in . . . . Be with them in bringing about change, and let them know that where the Spirit of the Lord is, there is freedom.

If the Son shall set us free, **we shall be free indeed.**

Life-giving God, one of your most characteristic actions is to give us personal freedom. We're addicted to so many things in our society – drugs, television, credit-card shopping, obsession with our size and shape. Above all we're addicted to doing our own thing and so resisting your loving purpose for us. We live lives of functional atheism and you long to release us into the freedom of Christ. Help us to live lives of faithful joy that draw others to the One we follow. May our lives be so freely shared that others will want to share that freedom. In silence Lord, we offer ourselves to you for you to reclaim the inner citadel of our lives and make us your own . . . *(pause)*. We are not our own but yours; put us to what you will. For . . .

. . . if the Son shall set us free, **we shall be free indeed.**

Life-giving God, one of your most characteristic actions is to bring the freedom of healing to the sick, and comfort to the bereaved. Give the assurance of your loving and healing presence to these people who are on our hearts as a community . . . *(list of sick and bereaved people)*. May these your children experience the freedom of your near presence and your healing love.

If the Son shall set us free, **we shall be free indeed.**

Life-giving God, in the freedom of your Spirit bring us, and all for whom we have prayed, to the freedom of your kingdom, and the light of everlasting day, for we ask it in the name of Jesus, our true and living Lord.

(21) A WORLD OF DIFFERENCE

One experience common to our globalized culture is that of diversity. This is sometimes perceived as threat and sometimes as opportunity. But the theme is important for prayer because we need to foster the conviction that life is not monochrome and we need to respect, enjoy and pray for the diverse ways men and women express their enthusiasm for life.

O God, we thank you for creating a world of difference.

When we travel we see the difference: weather, landscape and language, dress, food and political systems, the way people shop and sing and pray – everything is different, except smiles and laughter, a parent's touch and a lover's kiss. Help us to see 'difference' and not 'inferiority'. Help us to see opportunity and not threat. Help us to be enriched by different cultures and not made anxious by the realization that we are often a minority. Especially we pray for mutual respect between . . . and . . . (*Israelis and Palestinians, Christians and Muslims, etc.*).

Lord, hear us. **Lord, graciously hear us.**

When we watch the news or even talk to friends, we hear the difference in the way people see the world or want to change it. And sometimes we're astonished. How could they be so different? Which easily means, how could they be so wrong? Give us, Lord, humility in the face of difference, a concern to listen, and confidence to talk it through. Especially we pray for the current debate over . . . (*education, the health service, stem-cell research, gay relationships, etc.*). Help us to trust deeply that the truth will set us free.

Lord, hear us. **Lord, graciously hear us.**

When we talk to our fellow Christians we hear the difference in the way they approach the mystery and majesty of faith. We believe different things about you; we worship in every way from silent to sensational; we pray across the spectrum of spirituality; we put political commitment at the centre or way out on the edge; we order our churches as global communions or as local groups of friends. But this is the Body of Christ – colourful, diverse, sane, wild and off the wall. Give us, Lord, such enjoyment of, and respect for, each other that people may still say, 'See how these Christians love one another.' Especially may that be the case here in our own community with . . . *(other local churches)* and here in our own church.

Lord, hear us. **Lord, graciously hear us.**

When we listen to ourselves we hear many voices. Inside us is a community of views, a competition of personal agendas, sometimes even a civil war of desires. Help us to be merciful to our confusions and to listen compassionately to our own hearts. Especially we pray for your wisdom and grace in our ongoing personal dilemmas which we name before you silently now . . . .

Lord, hear us. **Lord, graciously hear us.**

O God, you have made a world of difference with a world of different people. We are each made in your image but are rarely of one mind. Let this be a source of inspiration and excitement to us as we explore the rich diversity of our humanity – a humanity you have taken on yourself, and brought into harmony, in Jesus Christ our Lord.

(22) WE LIGHT A CANDLE . . .

If we grant that we carry images around in our heads more than concepts, it follows that prayers with a strong central image will give people a powerful vehicle for their own prayer. The use of candles is well established as one of the most potent symbolic actions in prayer, so in the following intercession the phrase 'we light a candle . . .' can allow people to light their own candle mentally, or the words can be accompanied by the actual lighting of a candle.

In many churches today we find candle-stands for people to light a candle as an act of prayer. So now *(in our mind's eye)* we light candles for the world, for others and for ourselves, remembering the promise of Jesus, 'I am the light of the world.' 'The light shines in the darkness and the darkness has never put it out.'

To the words 'Lord, be light in the darkness', please respond **'steady and strong, clear and true'**.

Lord, we light a candle for peace in a world of broken promises. Let your light shine in . . . , where we heard again this week words of violence and the drums of war. Be a beacon of hope to those who despair and a warming fire to those who are weary.

Lord, be light in the darkness, **steady and strong, clear and true.**

We light a candle of hope for families and friends who are special to us. We think of a particular person, or couple, or relationship where we want your light to shine with hope, or healing, or forgiveness, or celebration . . . *(pause)*. These are your people; this is your light; please put them together.

Lord, be light in the darkness, **steady and strong, clear and true.**

We light a candle for guidance for people who have lost their way.
Many have been left behind in the race to acquire and accumulate,
to be fashionable or famous. Many have found life too complex
and are gradually giving up. Some people we know are struggling
at this moment and we hold them before you now . . . *(pause)*. Be
their pole star, their pillar of fire, their one true light – and hold
them to a true course and a worthy goal.

Lord, be light in the darkness, **steady and strong, clear and true.**

We light a candle for ourselves as we face particular issues this
week. Perhaps only we know the questions we face and the high
wire we must walk. Decisions that can't be put off much longer,
pressures that are becoming overwhelming, people we simply
must pick up and love. Be our light in the midst of these
problems – steady and strong, clear and true – as we worry and
waver before you. In silence now, we name our own particular
pressures . . . *(pause)*.

Lord, be light in the darkness, **steady and strong, clear and true.**

O God, we light candles for peace, for hope, for guidance;
candles for joy and thanksgiving and giving birth. We light
candles for dreaming and candles for dying. Light again in our
hearts, we pray, the candle of your love, as a light we can cherish
and share until we are overtaken by eternity. This we ask through
Jesus Christ our Lord.

(23) SOMEWHERE NEARBY

If our prayer is going to connect with the world we're part of for the other 167 hours a week when we aren't in church, we need to remember the raw-edged realities around us and not domesticate them into tidy, bland packages. These intercessions need to be adapted to make sense of our own local community, although we might be surprised at how many of these scenarios are present beneath the surface of the most ordinary-looking communities.

Today we pray for things happening very close to us but often unseen, unnoticed and unprayed-for. In the face of this hidden world, Lord, give us eyes to see and ears to hear.

Somewhere near us, at this moment, someone is ill and struggling
    to stay alive,
someone is struggling to keep their marriage together,
someone is struggling to resist a deep, familiar temptation.
Let's pray for them in their struggle . . . *(pause).*

Somewhere near us, at this moment, a football match is under
    way,
a couple are enjoying their new baby,
a family are planning their holidays,
a man is getting out his tools for today's DIY.
Let's pray for them in their relaxation . . . *(pause).*

Somewhere near us, at this moment, the air is electric with a
    family argument,
a young person is planning his/her next drug use,
a woman with depression is weeping quietly,
a man is feeling overwhelmed at the thought of work again on
    Monday.
Let's pray for them in their dark places . . . *(pause).*

Somewhere near us, at this moment, a woman has just finished
    reading a book that delighted her,
someone is working on a wood carving,
someone is learning lines for a play,
someone is downloading digital photos of their grandchildren.
Let's pray for them all in their creativity . . . *(pause)*.

Somewhere near us, at this moment, God the Father is holding
    the world on course,
God the Son is pulling together the wonderful raw material of
    human lives,
God the Holy Spirit is energizing his holy and unholy people.

Somewhere near us, at this moment, and every moment until
we're here again next week, God will be lovingly present to every
part of his creation, and every person in it. And he'll be struggling
with us, and shaping us; he'll be encouraging us and persuading
us; he'll be delighting in us and despairing over us. But he'll never
give up. And because he's inexhaustible, in the end he'll always
succeed.

Father, help us to trust you with your world, for Jesus' sake.

(24) THE PRAYER JESUS TAUGHT US

The Lord's Prayer is prayed millions of times every day. The problem is to mean what we pray! But Jesus was giving his disciples a framework for prayer which we do well to explore thoroughly all our lives and in all our praying. There are other places in this book where we look at how to use the Lord's Prayer in different contexts, but here we simply look at it as a framework for our intercession.

VOICE 1 Our Father in heaven

VOICE 2 Father, thank you for the privilege of calling you that – Father, Dad, a really close word. Obviously Jesus could call you that, but now we can too – which makes Jesus our older brother. As we continue to practise calling you Father, make us more like our older brother, more like Jesus. Maybe practice will make perfect – our Father in heaven.

VOICE 1 Hallowed be your name

VOICE 2 May your name be holy, and recognized as holy, all over the place. Our society regards many strange things as holy, or worthy of worship – money, sex and power, for example. We pray that the mystery of your holy presence may slip through all our defences and catch us unprepared. Yes, hallowed be your name.

VOICE 1 Your kingdom come, on earth as it is in heaven.

VOICE 2 This must be the most exciting prayer in the world! We pray for a time when your reign of justice, peace and love will make this world sparkle with your life. Help us to spot the kingdom coming, and to join in with

52

everything we've got. Yes, your kingdom come on earth – as it is in heaven.

VOICE 1 Give us this day our daily bread.

VOICE 2 Father, in your kingdom everyone will have what they need – their particular 'bread'. In anticipation of that time, we dare to ask for what we need – what we really need, not what we'd rather like to have. But even as we pray that prayer, we have to bring with us the hungry of the world whose need is simply bread, basic food, clean water, and a chance in life. We pray for our hungry neighbour. Give us *all* this day our daily bread.

VOICE 1 Forgive us our sins, as we forgive those who sin against us.

VOICE 2 Father, we know that much sin is love which has been misdirected onto the wrong things. You long to redirect our love to each other and to you. Help us to be open to your rich and reckless forgiveness. But make us aware too of those people we aren't forgiving, and against whom we still hold grudges. Bring them to our minds now and release them from our grasp . . . *(pause)*. Forgive us our sins, as we forgive those who sin against us.

VOICE 1 Lead us not into temptation, but deliver us from evil.

VOICE 2 It's not so much the minor infringements you're bothered about, Lord; it's the habits of the heart. You deeply desire that we shouldn't be taken into the clutches of the much greater darkness that opposes your reign of love at every turn. Rescue those who are playing with the darkness; keep a guard on their heart, a watch on their door, especially anyone we feel is particularly under pressure right now . . . *(pause)*. Lead us not into temptation, but deliver us from evil.

VOICE 1 For the kingdom, the power and the glory are yours, now and for ever.

VOICE 2 Thank goodness! The outcome of our struggles isn't in doubt. Following Christ may be hard, but it's not as hard as following nobody, or trying to follow ourselves! Where Christians are struggling today – in countries where religious repression is normal, or even in this country where many congregations are small and confidence is low – raise the eyes of your people to the coming dawn, for nothing can hold back your reign. For the kingdom, the power and the glory are yours, now and forever.

VOICE 1 Amen, Lord, amen

VOICE 2 Amen, Lord, amen.

(25) RENEW THE FACE OF THE EARTH

Christians believe in a God who's committed to making all things new (Revelation 21.5). Every Sunday is a celebration of the key to that process of renewal– the resurrection of Jesus Christ. Our intercessions therefore can echo that great theme, taking its implications into every area of human experience.

To the words 'Send forth your Spirit, Lord', please respond '**and renew the face of the earth**'.

God of our hearts and homes, thank you for your presence through this week in everything we've done. Some things we've done well; some things we've done badly. Some things we could show you; some things we'd rather not. We remember these things quietly now . . . . Take the rag-bag of our everyday experience, we pray, and work upon it with your patient grace, so transforming us bit by bit into the likeness of your Son, Jesus Christ.

Send forth your Spirit, Lord, **and renew the face of the earth.**

God of our health and happiness, we know you're committed to our being well, and to our well-being. We pray for those we know who are ill, lost or lonely, or facing some other major problem. These people we name in our hearts in silence now . . . . We pray that they and we may find health and healing on our journey to you.

Send forth your Spirit, Lord, **and renew the face of the earth.**

God of our town (*village/city*) and of our nation, thank you for those men and women who give themselves in politics and civic life to the renewal of our communities. They are often your agents of change while the rest of us sit at home and complain.

55

Help us, Lord, to do as St Paul said, and to recognize in local and national politics whatever is true, whatever is noble, whatever is right, whatever is pure, whatever is lovely – and to see it as part of your good plan and purpose to make all things new.

Send forth your Spirit, Lord, **and renew the face of the earth.**

God of our resilient but damaged world, we have survived so much of our own stupidity in war and greed and the abuse of our planet. Particularly we think of . . . (*issues in the news*). And all the time you are asking us to enlist in your kingdom – the better world that both lies within, and surrounds, our own. Help us to live as true citizens of that homeland, and to make the case for peace and justice and care for the good earth in every corner of the Kingdom.

Send forth your Spirit, Lord, **and renew the face of the earth.**

God of the universe, your renewing Spirit refreshes the farthest shores of creation. You never rest from your endless purpose of bringing all things together in Christ. In the Cross we see your pain as we resist your love; in the resurrection we see your inexhaustible life. Help us Lord, this week, to live, as far as lies in us, in the energy and joy of the resurrection. So may our lives contribute to that glorious goal, as you . . .

send forth your Spirit, Lord, **and renew the face of the earth.**

(26) DOORS

Sometimes a common image with a range of interpretations can provide a helpful peg for intercession. The visual reinforces the aural. Here the image of doors takes the intercession into both familiar and unfamiliar territory. The biblical echoes are of Jesus as the gate of the sheepfold, allowing sheep to go in and out in safety (John 10.9), and Jesus as the Way, taking us forward in our journey into God (John 14.6). Many customized additions, replacements and developments can be employed using this basic idea. A pause for reflection is advisable after each main petition and before the responsory.

Throughout our lives we go through doors. Some of these lead into good places; some into bad. Some give us hope; some cause anxiety. Let's pray for people going through doors into new places this day.

The response to the words 'Lord, you are the Way' is '**Lead us into your kingdom**'.

Father, we pray for people who are facing a door marked 'Push', but are unable to push because they have no strength left, or courage, or hope . . . .

Lord, you are the Way. **Lead us into your kingdom.**

We pray for people who are facing a door marked 'Private', and feeling they're always left outside, ignored, rejected or unnoticed . . . .

Lord, you are the Way. **Lead us into your kingdom.**

We pray for people facing a door marked 'Staff Only' but are unable to get a job because they've tried for hundreds of jobs and now have no confidence left . . . .

Lord, you are the Way. **Lead us into your kingdom.**

We pray for people facing a door that says 'Automatic' but whose experience is anything but that; they've have to fight for everything they've got . . . .

Lord, you are the Way. **Lead us into your kingdom.**

We pray for people facing a door marked 'Disabled', and immediately feeling identified as second class, an exception, or a problem . . . .

Lord, you are the Way. **Lead us into your kingdom.**

We pray for people facing a door marked 'Changing Rooms', wondering if they've got to change to be acceptable, and what the rules are, and who makes them . . . .

Lord, you are the Way. **Lead us into your kingdom.**

We pray for people facing a door marked 'Entrance', and wondering about the risks and opportunities of following Christ, what it would mean and what it would cost . . . .

Gracious God, you are the Way through many doors into a bigger place and a more sacred world. As we and others stand before many different doors throughout our lives, give us the confidence to knock, to enter, and to find freedom – in Jesus Christ our Lord.

(27) SPACE

An evocative image for our prayers can be that of space. The search for space in our lives is paralleled by our search for life in outer space; society is recognizing the need for 'personal' space, even sacred space, but nations are very reluctant to give space to refugees and others seeking a place to lay their heads. If the theme looks promising, use it! Better still – adapt it!

Father we come to church for many reasons, but one reason is often that we want some space in a crowded week, space to put things into perspective, space to be still, to slow down, and touch base. Space to be me. Space for you. Thank you for the gift of space you give us in this place. We've come to enjoy that space for a while together, and we do so now, in silence . . . *(pause of reasonable length)*.

We live in a society desperately chasing its tail, where life is full of more and more choices, more and more pressures – and more and more casualties. People can't keep up. Stress-related illnesses, depression, addictions, broken relationships, mental illness – all the statistics are up. But you, Lord, are a God of perfect timing and ample space. We'd love to walk at your pace, savouring every present moment and every holy encounter with others. We ask, therefore, not only for space for ourselves but also for one or two other people who are in need of that gift. Silently we name those people, holding them in the spaciousness of your love . . . *(pause)*.

Our church could be a gift to so many. This is sacred space, prayed in so much that it smells of holiness. Show us, Lord, how to make this special place more available to others, more a place of hospitality and welcome, where people may come, hopeful and unafraid, and where untold spaces may open up for all who enter. Show us how to help people come through the door, and how to greet them *as Christ* for us. In the quiet, now, make us aware of

the silent music of this place as we listen, and wait, and pray . . .
(*pause*).

Our cities teem with life. Many people are hardly ever alone,
rarely see much grass, and never hear the silence that supports the
universe. And yet they long for their own space, where they can
flourish and grow and welcome others. We pray for town
planners, architects, and those who design public spaces; may
they be aware of the deep longings of the heart to open up and
reach out and have space to fly. We pray for those in our
(*community/town/city*) who carry this opportunity and
responsibility. They could be your agents – we pray that they may
be just that . . . *(pause)*.

Lord, above, beyond and around us, the universe extends into
unimaginable space. And this can only expand our understanding
of you, for you hold all things in being, sustaining the universe.
Courageously, there are men and women who fly in space, and
scientists who apply their minds to mysteries that teeter on the
edge of comprehension. We pray for them as they push out the
boundaries of knowledge, reading your script, pursuing the clues
you've wrapped up in the wonders of the universe. Save us from
arrogance, and equip us for wonder . . . *(pause)*.

Lord of the immensity of outer space and the detail of every space
on earth, hold us moment by moment in the particular space of
our own lives. Help us to celebrate every moment of life until our
time and space is folded into the embrace of eternity, where you
reign forever, through Jesus Christ our Lord.

(28) IF ANYONE IS IN CHRIST . . .

The attempt in this intercession is to use a powerful biblical text as a refrain, and to emphasize it even more by using it as a double refrain. Clearly this will need understanding by the congregation, so either the response should be printed on the news-sheet or clear instructions given at the start – or both! Because of the number of words in these prayers, they are best read by two or more voices, possibly from different places around the church.

The response to the words 'If anyone is in Christ' is '**there is a new creation**'.

To the words 'The old has passed away', please respond '**behold the new has come**'.

If anyone is in Christ, **there is a new creation.**
The old has passed away, **behold the new has come.**

Voice 1

Lord, so easily we forget in our churches that we are a new creation. The struggle goes on to find Sunday School teachers, to repair the roof, to pay the quota. Too easily the vision fades, and the Christian story which brought us to life becomes a suffocating system that leads us back to captivity. Lord, remind us again and again that it need not be so, that there is a new world and we are part of it. Help us to take from your hands each day the gift of new life.

If anyone is in Christ, **there is a new creation.**
The old has passed away, **behold the new has come.**

Voice 2

Lord, our world is old and spiritually tired. We have forgotten the ways that lead to peace. We have forgotten to do justice, to love mercy, and to walk humbly with you. Restrain the forces of cruelty and exploitation, and strengthen with your costly love

61

those who struggle for a new social order. Remind us again and again that there is a new world and we are part of it. Help us to take from your hands each day the gift of new life.
If anyone is in Christ, **there is a new creation.**
The old has passed away, **behold the new has come.**

Voice 1

Lord, there are people living around us who are in a bad way. Within a few hundred yards of where most of us live there are people with cancer, depression and crippling loneliness. Others are feeling betrayed by a partner; some are frightened for their children; some are in the grip of irrational phobias. Bring them your comfort and healing. Stir us to simple acts of kindness and generosity. And by whatever means, put in the hearts of those who suffer the glimmer of a belief that it need not be so, that there is a new world and they can be part of it. Help us to take from your hands each day the gift of new life.

If anyone is in Christ, **there is a new creation.**
The old has passed away, **behold the new has come.**

Voice 2

Lord, we have caught sight of this new creation. We glimpsed it in a crisp summer's dawn, in a family party, in a lover's touch, in a prodigal son returned. And we have seen this new creation full-bodied in the risen Christ. What we have glimpsed, we celebrate this morning (at this resurrection meal). Help us to live out the values and commitments of the new creation and give us joy and confidence as ambassadors for Christ in this new world of which we are part.

If anyone is in Christ, **there is a new creation.**
The old has passed away, **behold the new has come.**

So be it. Amen.

2 INTERCESSIONS AT FESTIVALS AND SPECIAL OCCASIONS

PRACTICALITIES

This is a checklist of things to consider when preparing intercessions for festivals and special events in the life of the church.

1   Try to capture the essence of the festival. Go to the heart of what the festival means, and make sure that meaning stands at the centre of the intercessions, however they are expressed.

2   Find a controlling theme around which to wind the intercessions. This may often be expressed in the responsory. In the examples that follow, Christmas has a holding theme of light, Easter has the theme of the Emmaus story, Remembrance Sunday uses the poppy, and so on.

3   Remember the different groups of people who might be there. Quite different 'clientele' may be present on these special Sundays, and their needs must be taken into account in terms of what they may understand, expect and value. Large numbers of occasional churchgoers may be there at Christmas, more families from the local school on Mothering Sunday ('Mothers' Day'!), the British Legion on Remembrance Sunday. And probably only the core faithful will be there on Ascension Day or Ash Wednesday. Our prayers must be sensitive to the particular congregation.

4   Be careful to introduce any expectations. For example, introduce a responsory with extra care or lead into a time of silence with quite clear suggestions of what to do with this time.

5 Be prepared to be briefer than usual. There is often some other activity which is appropriate to the festival or special occasion, and time will be at a premium. We mustn't sell our intercessions short but we have to consider the overall length of the service.

6 Be aware of the potential for evangelism. This is a 'shop window' service for the church, so really careful preparation is important.

(29) ADVENT

Advent is that time of longing, hoping and waiting that our culture finds so hard to understand. Ours is a world of instant satisfactions, and the delay implicit in longing, hoping and waiting is an alien idea. It's the more important therefore that Christians shouldn't compromise the rich themes of Advent by letting Christmas take over too soon.

The response to the words 'Your kingdom come' is '**Your will be done**'.

Holy God, ever with us and ever on your way towards us, we look to you this Advent, willing your kingdom to come, but knowing it's not ours to take. So come to us in the many guises of love; meet our longing; enter our waiting; give life to our hoping.

Your kingdom come. **Your will be done.**

Advent God, Hope of the hopeless, you alone give us reason to go on. Give hope to those who this day all over the world are hungry for basic gifts – food to stop the children aching with hunger, a home to put pictures on the wall, education to open the door to a job, justice to give everyone a chance. We particularly pray for . . . and . . . *(places in the news, campaigns for justice, people we know working abroad, etc.)*. God of hope, give hope to the hopeless.

Your kingdom come. **Your will be done.**

Advent God, Love of the loveless, you are the One who never fails to love to the limit. You love without question the loveless, the unlovely and the unlovable. May we do the same. We're aware of people or groups of people whom we instinctively reject because of what they've done to us or what they represent to us. We identify them in our hearts right now . . . (*pause*). Give us strength to love; give them strength to respond. And give us the gentleness to love ourselves as well. God of love, give love to the loveless.

Your kingdom come. **Your will be done.**

Advent God, Joy of the joyless, you are the source of inexhaustible delight. In a world of desperate pleasure and stale smiles, take us to the place where true joys are to be found. We pray for those who face Christmas and the New Year with deep apprehension, knowing it to be a time where much true poverty is revealed – poverty of love, of friends, of purpose, of spirit. In silence, we pray for particular families – including even our own . . . (*pause*). God of joy, give joy to the joyless.

Your kingdom come. **Your will be done.**

Advent God, God of those who think themselves godless, you are the rock on which our lives are built. Have mercy on those who try to live without you and lead them gently to the truth that sets us free. Come afresh to the minds of those who think they've thought their way out of your reach. Come afresh too to those of us who think we have it all taped, for whom your mystery and power have become dulled and routine. Come afresh to the hearts of us all, whether they be full of distractions or swept clean and empty. We long for you to be central to our lives, and central to the life of the world.

Your kingdom come. **Your will be done.**

Holy God, this Advent we set ourselves to longing again – longing and waiting and hoping. We long for your kingdom to come and for this world to be transformed, for it to be on earth as it is in heaven. But the glimmerings of that new world have also to become real in us. So come, our Advent God, with the promise of a new birth, in Jesus Christ our Lord. Amen.

(30) CHRISTMAS

Christmas can be a time of extraordinary hope and considerable despair. It focuses many memories and emotions. Public prayer, therefore, needs to be both celebratory and sensitive to these complexities.

The response to the words 'In this season of light' is '**be light for the world**'.

In this season of gifts, we celebrate your coming as the only gift we really need. As we enjoy the surprises and the imagination of those who give us presents, may the child in the straw be the gift that really overwhelms us. And may our giving to others flow from hearts motivated by gratitude for *your* glorious gift.

In this season of light, **be light for the world.**

In this season of family gatherings, we celebrate your coming to be part of a human family. As we experience the delights and the frustrations of family life this Christmas, may the child in the straw be the still life who holds us together. And may our care for each other reflect your profound care for us all.

In this season of light, **be light for the world.**

In this season of memories, we celebrate our corporate memory of your arrival in darkness, a sharp cry in the night air, animals shuffling nearby, rough shepherds from the hills, a star, strange visitors from the east. And our own individual memories take us back to distant times of greater innocence and less cluttered lives, of other relationships and different places. May the child in the straw be the continuity we need, the thread of gold that holds past and present in a single story.

67

In this season of light, **be light for the world.**

In this season of peace, we celebrate the peacemakers who listen to the angels' song and seek to bring peace to your people on earth. And yet we stand on the vulnerable edge of violence in many parts of the world; especially we remember . . . and . . . . May the child in the straw be a reminder of another way and a greater light, one that unites every race under heaven.

In this season of light, **be light for the world.**

In this season of hope, we celebrate your coming like the dawn after a long night. As we struggle with our personal darkness, the issues and conflicts, the temptations and confusions, so may the child in the straw draw us into a larger and safer space, where complexity dissolves into simplicity, and your light shines for ever.

In this season of light, **be light for the world.**

Lord of light, you have come to draw us out of darkness into your glorious light. We come to you afresh this Christmas, longing for a new start and another chance. Take our Christmas celebrations and fill them with golden, glowing hope to sustain us through this coming year. We ask this in the new-born name of Jesus Christ our Lord.

(31) NEW YEAR

New Year is a time of reflection. It focuses our memories and our hopes. It may also be a time of some anxiety – what will happen in this coming year, given that each year seems to throw up its share of crises? How can we start again? How can we get it right this time? Prayers at this time therefore need to have a thoughtful character and to give sufficient time for different parts of our lives to be brought before God. As ever, be prepared to adapt this prayer to fit your local context, for example in the questions you put.

To the words 'Lord for the years', the response is '**we give our thanks and praise**'.

We come before God at the end of the year, conscious of many memories, thoughts and feelings. We look back at times bathed in sunlight, and other times cast in shadow. We see faces and places, times and seasons, love and loss. We offer God our memories . . .

What gave us most pleasure this last year? . . .

What do we want to put behind us? . . .

Gracious God, this last year has been well filled. Thank you for your quiet, solid presence through every part of it, rejoicing with us, weeping with us, loving, persuading, nudging, comforting.

Lord, for the years, **we give our thanks and praise.**

As the year tips over into 200(?) we look down the slope into the new year with both eagerness and anxiety. This year could hold so much that would be wonderful, but we're never more than a phone-call away from a crisis. We offer God our hopes at the birth of the year . . .

What do we most long for this year? . . .

What do we intend to do differently this year? . . .

Gracious God, you hold the coming year in the palm of your hand, not to control but to cherish. You promise that your love will be inexhaustible, and that you'll work at full stretch for our well-being. Thank you for those good promises to remember and to claim afresh each day.

Lord for the years, **we give our thanks and praise.**

And for the world around us, we hold our breath. So much to desire, so much to fear. But the better way is surely this: so much to pray for, so much to work for.

What places are most in need of peace and hope? . . .

What world leaders are most in need of our prayers? . . .

Gracious God, it is your will to hold together the nations of the earth in a single peace. Let the imprint of your love be seen in every troubled country. Let the earth breathe more freely at the end of the coming year. And may we have made our own contribution to the earth's freedom.

Lord of the years, **we give our thanks and praise.**

Lord of *this* year, we give you our faith, and our hunger for the Kingdom. Amen

(32) A HOLY LENT

Lent is a time of preparation, discipline and guilt in about equal measure. We prepare for the central memories and festivals of the faith, we discipline ourselves to show we mean business, and then we fail to keep to the disciplines! But we hear from God a serious call to a holy life and it's important to face the challenge. These intercessions try to be realistic but hopeful. A short but significant pause can be employed between each paragraph to allow some 'owning' and appropriation of the general theme.

Please feel free to join in with the words '**Good Lord deliver us**'.

Good Lord, in this season of Lent, help us to aim high as we seek to renew the discipline of our discipleship. May we take up the best and give up the rest, and know your mercy and grace in all things.

From all self-seeking, self-promotion and self-indulgence;
from all self-pity, self-glorification and selfishness;
from all self-hatred, self-harm and self-destruction,
Good Lord deliver us.

From all that would keep us from going to church;
from all that would stop us from reading your word;
from all that would keep us from receiving the sacrament,
Good Lord deliver us.

From the laziness that would stop us before we begin;
from the carelessness that would mean we would do it badly;
from the impatience that would mean we wouldn't finish,
Good Lord deliver us.

From all that would limit our loving of our neighbour;
from all that would limit our loving of God;
from all that would spoil our attempt to be good,
Good Lord deliver us.

By the disciplines of Lent and the encouragement of others;
by the Body of Christ and the sharing of lives;
by the desire of our hearts and the need of our souls,
Good Lord deliver us.

By your agony and trial;
by your cross and passion;
by your mighty resurrection and glorious ascension,
Good Lord deliver us.

By all that we attempt, strengthened by you;
by all that we long for, fed by you;
by all that is in us, blessed by you,
Good Lord deliver us.

In every ordinary day of Lent;
in every temptation to follow the crowd;
in every attempt to justify our compromises,
Good Lord deliver us.

Give us Lord the blessings of a holy Lent, true journeying in Holy
Week, and give us a holy and glorious Easter.
Give us time to receive your teaching and to amend our lives,
give us faith to be open to the graceful filling of your Holy Spirit,
and finally give us leave to come to your eternal joy.

Holy God,
Holy and strong,
Holy and immortal,
have mercy on us.

(33) MOTHERING SUNDAY/BAPTISM

With some adaptation these intercessions can be used for either Mothering Sunday or a service which includes a baptism. The holding theme is Mary's Magnificat (Luke 1.46–55), which would need to be read or used previously in the service. It should then be referred to in the introduction to the prayers.

Our prayers today pick up themes from Mary's Song (the Magnificat) where Mary was expressing her delight in her unexpected pregnancy.

Gracious Father, on this *(Mothering Sunday/Baptism Sunday)* we give thanks for the unique privilege of having children to bring up. We feel so unprepared; we feel such a responsibility; we often feel so overwhelmed. Help us to rest in the knowledge that we could be asked to do no more important thing than to love, guide and nurture a new life. In doing this we're sharing in your divine activity of loving, guiding and nurturing the whole human race.

And so we pray with Mary:

'My soul proclaims the greatness of the Lord, and my spirit rejoices in God my Saviour.'

Lord, hear us. **Lord, graciously hear us.**

We pray for mothers everywhere:

- young mothers overawed by the task, and by the depth of their feelings;
- older mothers thrilled beyond measure that at last a child has come;
- mothers in Britain who are single, scared and poor;
- mothers in many developing countries whose diet is thin and whose milk is scarce.

Hasten the day when mothers everywhere can say with Mary,

'The Mighty One has done great things for me, and holy is his name.'

Lord, hear us. **Lord, graciously hear us.**

We pray for fathers everywhere:

- young fathers, unsure how to be a father and a husband, a lover and a friend;
- fathers in poorer countries wondering how to feed yet another child;
- fathers in the Western world, leaving home too early and coming home too late to share these special years.

Hasten the day when fathers everywhere can say,

'His mercy is for those who fear him, from generation to generation.'

Lord, hear us. **Lord, graciously hear us.**

We pray for couples everywhere who are without children:

- those who've made the choice and are happy;
- those who've not made that choice and are desperate for a child;
- those who are seeking help and waiting anxiously, month by month;
- those who are trying to adopt, and going through a long process.

Hasten the day when all who want children can say,

'He has shown strength with his arm, and lifted up the lowly.'

Lord, hear us. **Lord, graciously hear us.**

Mothering Sunday

We pray for the family lives of the nation, upon which so much depends. We know that good experience of family life leads to good family life in the next generation. Be among us to bless, guide and keep safe these special units of love, patience and forgiveness. And continue to teach us the way of Jesus, who knew the security of a loving home with Mary and Joseph in Nazareth. So may we all come to say with Mary,

'My soul proclaims the greatness of the Lord, and my spirit rejoices in God my Saviour.'

Baptism Sunday

We pray for *(these children)* baptized today in our midst. As *(they)* embark on *(their)* life in the Church, may *(they)* know here as well as at home, the security that Jesus knew in the loving home of Mary and Joseph in Nazareth. So may *(they)* also come to say with Mary,

'My soul proclaims the greatness of the Lord, and my spirit rejoices in God my Saviour.'

Lord, hear us. **Lord, graciously hear us.**

So receive our prayers and bless our best efforts, which we offer in Jesus' name.

Amen.

(34) HOLY WEEK

This form of prayer is suitable for any day in Holy Week, including Good Friday. It uses one of the powerful images of the week – that of the gradual darkening of the atmosphere as fear and betrayal leave Jesus finally alone, the last light in the darkness, until that too is extinguished. Obviously this could be symbolized by the actual extinguishing of candles as the prayer proceeds, or it may be left up to the imagination of the people praying. While not strictly intercession, it is nevertheless prayer for all of us present and, by extension, for all of humankind in need of God's mercy.

The response to the words 'Lord have mercy' is '**Christ have mercy**'.

Jesus, the candles shone brightly on Palm Sunday. This was a day of festival and welcome. Only you knew that the truth lay elsewhere.

Jesus, hold us in your truth.

Lord have mercy. **Christ have mercy.**

You taught passionately in the temple, offering the word of life, but you were hemmed in by the small-minded leaders of the people with their petty arguments about marriages in heaven and paying taxes to Caesar.

Jesus, save us from triviality.

Lord have mercy. **Christ have mercy.** *(First candle goes out.)*

You accepted the loving touch and anointing of a wise and wounded woman, but there were none thereafter who would care for your body. Only those who would hurt it.

Jesus, make us compassionate in all our ways.

Lord have mercy. **Christ have mercy.** *(Next candle goes out.)*

You had supper with your friends and even gave Judas the seat of honour, but he it was who slipped out into the night and finished supper with the devil.

Jesus, save us from delusion and deceit.

Lord have mercy. **Christ have mercy.** *(Next candle goes out.)*

You hugged the ground in Gethsemane in an agony of faith and doubt, but your three best friends left you to it. While the future of the world was in the balance, they fell asleep.

Jesus, keep us loyal and true in all our relationships.

Lord have mercy. **Christ have mercy.** *(Next candle goes out.)*

Peter and John followed you to the High Priest's house, and there by the charcoal fire Peter denied he'd ever met you. Peter – who had sworn an hour earlier that he was yours forever.

Jesus, give us courage to hold the faith under pressure.

Lord have mercy. **Christ have mercy.** *(Next candle goes out.)*

You were whipped half to death, humiliated before the crowd, friendless in a world of power and corruption. And then you heard the people's piercing cry: 'Crucify him!'

Jesus, keep us from foolishly following the crowd.

Lord have mercy. **Christ have mercy.** *(Next candle goes out.)*

You hung on that fierce cross, tortured within and without. The world you came to save had turned against you, and even heaven itself stayed silent in the darkest mystery of all. 'My God, my God, why have you forsaken me?'

Jesus, please save us from despair.

Lord have mercy. **Christ have mercy.** *(Next candle goes out.)*

And so came the end. You had drunk the dark wine of suffering to the dregs. There was nothing more to give, no more light to shine. 'It is finished.' The light of the world had gone out. *(Last candle goes out.)*

Silence

Lord of our stricken world, there is nothing we can do to redeem our blindness in sending you to your death. You only can redeem. But keep us in touch with the pain of the world, where you are still hung out to die, and there may we ease you from your cross, tend your wounds, and offer you the friendship we failed to give on a green hill far away. This we ask in sadness and hope, for your sake and for ours, Amen.

(35) EASTER AT EMMAUS

The Emmaus story in Luke 24 has enduring appeal in its humanity, its wonder and its mixture of simplicity and complexity. Obviously these prayers would work best if this Gospel reading has been used. The prayers follow the developing narrative of the story – a method which can be used with other biblical passages.

To the words 'The Lord is risen', please respond **'He is risen indeed. Alleluia!'**

Lord of the Emmaus road, thank you for this stunning good news! Like the two disciples on that road, we are often despondent. Our best plans and highest hopes evaporate and we're left with dust in our mouths on that weary journey back to where we started. And if not us, that experience may be familiar to a loved one at this moment. Walk with us, Lord; listen to our story; and then let us hear yours, straight from the empty tomb.

The Lord is risen. **He is risen indeed. Alleluia!**

Lord of the journey, you opened the Scriptures to those disciples as you walked, and their hearts burned within them. Help us to listen to the good news of Scripture, to read, mark, learn and inwardly digest it, so that our palates are not jaded with too much familiarity but rather inspired by the vitality and truth that we find there. Walk with us, Lord, and let us hear your story, straight from the empty tomb.

The Lord is risen. **He is risen indeed. Alleluia!**

Lord of the open door, you accepted the hospitality of strangers who urged you warmly to stay a while with them. May we show a similar enthusiasm to welcome the stranger, to open our homes, our churches and our country to those in need. And as we offer such hospitality may we find that we also have been blessed, for we have entertained *you* unawares. Sit with us, Lord, and let us hear your story, straight from the empty tomb.

The Lord is risen. **He is risen indeed. Alleluia!**

Lord of the broken bread and the blessed wine, you performed those familiar actions and the two disciples suddenly knew who you were. As we come to your table week by week, may we too know the shock of recognition and blessing, as you share the life that is in you and is available to us. Give us confidence to invite others to the banquet, in anticipation of the Meal at the End of the World in your heavenly kingdom. Preside at our table, Lord, and let us hear *and experience* your story, straight from the empty tomb.

The Lord is risen. **He is risen indeed. Alleluia!**
Alleluia indeed! Amen.

(36) ASCENSION

Because Ascension Day comes on a Thursday this great festival often gets sidelined. However, its theme of the Lordship of Christ over the kingdoms of this world is one that's particularly important to learn again. These intercessions take us to various arenas of human activity where the Lordship of Christ needs to be established.

The response to the words 'Jesus Christ is Lord' is **'to the glory of God the Father'**.

Lord, be the Ascended One in our church, where too many things of little importance can often distract us from the few things of major importance. When our vision is small and our faith is thin, remind us again of your towering beauty, reigning over all things. Give your church here such a vision of your glory that nothing on earth can compare, and nothing can tear us away from our faith.

Jesus Christ is Lord, **to the glory of God the Father.**

Lord, be the Ascended One in the community of nations. All around we see signs of violence, rumours of war and threats of terrorism. The world is running out of time to rescue Africa from Aids or indeed to save the planet from irreversible damage. Just recently we've learned that . . . *(news items that have caused concern)*. And yet there is another reality – a new world has already broken in, your kingdom is established just under the surface, and justice and peace are within our reach. Lord, help us to live in the old world and there proclaim your new kingdom.

Jesus Christ is Lord, **to the glory of God the Father.**

Lord, be the Ascended One in our own society. So often it feels as if our culture is tired, adrift in its own relativism, not knowing what to value and what to live by. We pray for those who

81

influence the health of our society – the government and Parliament, journalists and broadcasters, writers and film-makers, local councils and voluntary organizations. We pray in silence for any such people who get under our skin or we can see need our prayer . . . (*pause*); give to these men and women courage to stand for something, lest they fall for anything, and may that 'something' be good, just and true, in terms of your kingdom.

Jesus Christ is Lord, **to the glory of God the Father.**

Lord, be the Ascended One in our own hearts, for that's where the main struggle goes on. Be our Lord not in theory only but in daily application. Be Lord of our values at work, of the way we relate to our closest family, of the way we spend our money, of what we do when no one is looking. Be Lord of how we spend our time and how we vote, of how we handle our sexuality and how we approach difficult ethical issues. Be Lord of how we relate to the wider world and its needs, of how we sing and celebrate and enjoy this world's gifts. May we be able to say with joy,

Jesus Christ is Lord, **to the glory of God the Father.**
Now and in all eternity. Amen.

(37) PENTECOST

Pentecost lends itself to the use of its strong images, but other festivals and seasons of the year also have symbols attached to them which can be used to reinforce and enliven the intercessions. The response here would have to be introduced and rehearsed, or printed on the service sheet.

To the words 'With wind and fire from heaven', please respond **'Lord, energize your Church'**.

God of wind and fire, bring to us today the surprises of your Spirit. As we gather this Sunday like so many others, we may be shy or sluggish, tired or timid, and without expectation of a new birth. So come among us, burn up our fears in the heat of your love; blow through our minds with the joyous freedom of your Spirit. Make this church a crucible of love and joy, where your kingdom is coming.

With wind and fire from heaven, **Lord, energize your Church.**

God of foreign tongues, you have taken your message to the corners of the earth. Not just Parthians, Medes and Elamites, but Chinese, Nepalese and Korean. We pray for those who follow your *living* Word with the *written* word, those who translate the Bible, and interpret and teach the faith. In particular we pray for our linked mission partners in . . . . May we learn afresh from them about the vitality of churches filled with your living presence.

With wind and fire from heaven, **Lord, energize your Church.**

God of the Church, which was born this happy morning, make us powerful in proclamation, as Peter was powerful that first day of Pentecost when 3,000 people were baptized. As the massive fallout of that great day continues, so thousands of people start

83

the Christian journey every day all over the world. Make us a church here at . . . where people will also find new life and hope. Make us attractive as a church through the love and joy which spill out naturally from our faith and the way we live our lives.

With wind and fire from heaven, **Lord, energize your Church.**

God of the silence that followed the storm, we know you to be a God who acts where your people give you space and freedom to do so. We offer you that space now as we wait in silence for you to come to us, to speak to us, to be with us however you want . . . *(longer silence)*.

Lord, what we know not, teach us;
what we are not, make us;
what we dare not, inspire us to do,
as we pray:

With wind and fire from heaven, **Lord, energize your Church.**

(38) HARVEST

Harvest presents particular problems and opportunities. The traditional harvest festival locks into our rural nostalgia but may leave us feeling strangely disconnected from everyday concerns rather than fundamentally integrated into earthy realities, as it would have done in previous generations. We have to work harder to make the everyday connections, and use more imagination. In these intercessions items representing each part of the prayer can be brought forward and placed on the altar or an appropriate table – soil, cheese, fruit, wine, etc. The congregation should be encouraged to look, not to close their eyes.

To the words 'All things come from you', please respond '**and of your own do we give you**'.

Creator God, we make nothing from nothing, but only from what you give us. You are the source of all good things, and on you we depend. Give us eyes to see that truth and hearts to be thankful.

For all things come from you, **and of your own do we give you.**

We bring you topsoil, dark source of life and growth. In the mysterious exchanges of sun, soil and rain, you renew the fruitfulness of the earth. Bless this good earth so that it blesses us and we in turn bless each other with generosity and justice.

For all things come from you, **and of your own do we give you.**

We bring you produce from our dairies, and wool and leather from the animals with whom we share the earth. Help us to respect every life on earth and to care for the well-being of animals in birth, life and death. Especially we pray for due care of animals in transit and entirely dependent on our humanity.

For all things come from you, **and of your own do we give you.**

We bring you the harvest of fruits – rich, ripe and succulent. We stand amazed at the mesmerizing variety of the earth's fruitfulness and the tastes which delight us day by day. May we delight also in paying fair prices to producers in developing countries, knowing that fair trade is an aspect of a just world.

For all things come from you, **and of your own do we give you.**

We bring you the harvest of vegetables which fill our bodies with goodness and health. Give us wisdom not to pollute the earth and poison the ground that feeds us, but rather to respect and cherish the good things that surround us and on which we depend.

For all things come from you, **and of your own do we give you.**

We bring you the harvest of our cornfields, and the bread which feeds the world. Make us generous in a world where the poor are often sent away empty. Bread is basic. Wind and rain have caressed it; Jesus often blessed it; we need humility when we touch bread.

For all things come from you, **and of your own do we give you.**

We bring you the harvest of flowers and vineyards which bring beauty and pleasure to our leisured moments. Make us responsible in our consumption of the fruit of the vine. Sun and wind have caressed it; Jesus often blessed it; we need wisdom when we drink wine.

For all things come from you, **and of your own do we give you.**

We bring you the harvest of our inventiveness, the tools and machinery we use to process the gifts we receive from you. *(Bring up here an array of smaller tools, a food processor, or – failing everything – a few tins of food.)* We thank you for gifts of the mind, for knowledge, innovation and industry. May we always make it a principle and a priority to work with you and not against you in sustaining and redeeming your world.

For all things come from you, **and of your own do we give you.**

Loving, creator God, we have symbolically brought many things to you. We bring you one thing more – our humble, thankful hearts. Because, 'Yours, Lord, is the greatness, the power, the glory, the splendour and the majesty. Everything in heaven and on earth is yours. All things come from you, **and of your own do we give you.**

(39) REMEMBRANCE SUNDAY

*Interestingly, the annual act of remembrance seems to be gaining
in impact in recent years. Perhaps it's because those who have
direct memories are becoming fewer in number and we realize
what we're in danger of losing. Those who lead worship are faced
with the responsibility of making the memory vivid without being
too sentimental. Here is one way of doing that in intercession,
using a standard poppy with two petals and a leaf.*

As we pray today I invite you to use your poppy, either by
detaching it or holding it where it is. If you don't have a poppy
with you, please picture one in your mind.

First, we hold one of the petals of the poppy. Father, the red of
this petal is like the red of the blood shed by so many in the wars
of the last century. We remember members of our family who
were directly involved in those wars, some in the armed forces,
some left behind. We remember injury, trauma, death, courage,
fear – lives changed forever. We give thanks for so many who
were prepared to pay the highest price of all . . . .

Lord, in your mercy, **hear our prayer.**

Now we take hold of another petal on our poppy. In doing so, we
hold before God the violence and warfare of our own times – the
simmering violence in . . . , the open hostilities in . . . , the threat
of terrorism everywhere . . . . We pray, Father, that you will give
us politicians and military leaders equal to the huge tasks they
face – wise in judgement, calm in spirit, makers of peace.

Lord, in your mercy, **hear our prayer.**

Now we touch the centre of the poppy, the place where the seeds
are kept, ready for new life. Lord, take the seeds of peace which
lie in the hearts of your people everywhere, and cast them

generously over every continent and nation. Let those seeds germinate, grow and flourish, especially today in . . . . Beat our swords into ploughshares, our spears into pruning hooks and our weapons of mass destruction into technologies for peace.

Lord, in your mercy, **hear our prayer.**

Now we hold the green leaf (or the green stem) and remember the green and growing hope which comes from faith alone, faith in a God for whom everything is possible, even in the darkest hour. May hope guide our politics, our nation, our thinking and our lives. May hope draw us ever nearer to that day when the world shall be filled with the glory of God as the waters cover the sea.

Lord, in your mercy, **hear our prayer.**

In your mercy, forgive our foolish ways,
In your mercy, help us to listen before we fight,
In your mercy, hold back the men of war,
In your mercy, save the innocent,
In your mercy, hear us,
In your mercy,
In your mercy.

(40) ALL SAINTS (AT ANY TIME)

All Saints Day on 1 November isn't the only time to celebrate the saints of the Church, large and small, local and universal. But if this is the chosen time there's an interesting symbiosis between this remembrance and that of Guy Fawkes four days later! Familiar images from 'Bonfire Night' might heighten the impact of the saints.

The response to the words 'For all the saints who from their labours rest' is '**Thy name, O Jesus, be forever blest**'.

Father in heaven, you have gathered in your keeping and celebration the saints of the Church through the ages and from every nation. Not one is lost, and every one of them lights up the halls of heaven with their beauty and faithfulness. Thank you for the brightness of their witness to you and their inspiration to us.

For all the saints who from their labours rest,
Thy name, O Jesus, be forever blest.

Some of your saints have streaked like rockets into the night sky with power, light and colour. Peter, upon whom the Church is founded; Paul, who took the faith to the known world; Augustine, that great thinker, so far ahead of his time. Thank you for the audacity and the dazzling faith of these great saints. Keep the Church ever in awe of these men and women, and always ready to learn from them.

For all the saints who from their labours rest,
Thy name, O Jesus, be forever blest.

Others of your saints have exploded upon the Church and upon society like bangers on Bonfire Night. These prophets have told the truth, sparing no one, confronting both leaders and nations with the unchanging demands of justice and the never-ending

possibility of peace. Bonhoeffer and Martin Luther King, Nelson
Mandela and Desmond Tutu. Thank you for their courage that
few of us could ever show but all of us can recognize as divine.
May we be strengthened by these lives and empowered to face
our own lesser challenges.

For all the saints who from their labours rest,
Thy name, O Jesus, be forever blest.

And some there are – too many – who have paid the ultimate
price of faithful witness, and like Catherine on her wheel, have
died terribly before they entered your glory. We know the last
century saw more martyrs than any other, and we lament the
violence of the human beings you made for love. May we be kept
sober and alert by the sacrifices others have made, so that we may
never take our faith for granted, and always be ready to take a
stand.

For all the saints who from their labours rest,
Thy name, O Jesus, be forever blest.

And we remain – small sparklers in what can sometimes seem to
be immense darkness. Our light is sometimes brittle and short,
going out when we're least prepared. But we know there breaks a
yet more glorious day and our hesitant light will be swallowed up
in lasting glory. So keep us confident in the good that even our
meagre sparklers can do as we hold before friends and colleagues
the promise of your dazzling love.

For all the saints who from their labours rest,
Thy name, O Jesus, be forever blest.

As the bonfire dies down and the excitement of the fireworks
fades, the same may happen to our memories of the lives and
examples of the saints. So keep us, we pray, very much aware of
the noble line we have joined and the privilege of hanging on to
the back of the communion of saints. Enrich the poverty of our

love and commitment, inflame our hearts with the passion we once had; and keep us close to the fire from which all the saints have drawn their holiness – Jesus Christ our Lord.

3 INTERCESSIONS IN INFORMAL WORSHIP AND SMALL GROUPS

PRACTICALITIES

A checklist of principles to bear in mind when preparing intercessions for informal worship and small groups:

1 **Aim for participation.** This is an interactive age in which people are being brought up with participatory forms of learning. However, we must be aware of people's reluctance to break ingrained habits about 'what you do in church' and what you don't.

2 **Visual reinforcement.** In a visual culture we need to use a multi-sensory approach, rather than simply expect people to engage with the spoken word from the front.

3 **Beware of gimmicks.** The aim is to take our deepest concerns to the heart of God, not to prove how clever we can be. The trouble is that one person's gimmick is another person's imaginative master-stroke!

4 **Use appropriate vocabulary.** Neither too complex nor too juvenile. Language should be concrete but rich, down to earth but open to metaphor. A real art, learned by critical listening and honest feedback!

5 **Be brief.** Or at least, don't be long-winded. We need to engage people fully in the activity of praying, but too many leaders finish their prayers (or their sermons) but then don't stop!

6   Pray about real issues in the wider world. Don't settle for safe prayer for home, family, church and the sick. Pray for the ordinary or unpleasant realities of which people are aware. Show that every aspect of life is of concern to God.

7   Aim for a balance of familiarity and variety. Repeating familiar actions is the basis of much human enjoyment, from family rituals to TV game shows. But variety gives people new opportunities to enter and experience the vitality of prayer. Aim for a healthy balance.

8   Don't embarrass people. Don't put people on the spot or 'volunteer' them. Be confident and purposeful, and enough people will probably volunteer. Don't assume more faith than the fringe attender in fact has.

9   Don't be afraid of trying quiet periods of prayer. Even quite young children can be responsive to moments of attentive silence – but don't count on it!

10   Have a feedback mechanism. It's important to know if an approach to prayer was actually helpful or not. You may sense the answer, but others will be able to fill in the details.

(41) PALMS UP, PALMS DOWN

This is a way of getting started with a congregation or a group in prayer. It helps people to become aware of themselves and their concerns, and of God and his possibilities. It depends, as so often, on the confidence of the leader in not taking it too quickly but allowing the group time to engage with themselves and with God.

What to do

1 Ask people to close their eyes and to put their hands, palm upwards, on their laps. Ask them to become aware of all the issues and concerns they've brought with them, the unfinished business, the sticky relationships, the work awaiting them, the decisions that have to be taken. 'Hold all these things in your hands. Feel the weight of them. Recognize that they are part of you at this moment, and that you've brought them with you.' *Pause . . . .*

2 Ask people now to turn their hands over so that the palms are facing downwards on their laps. 'As you turn your palms over, feel all those issues and concerns slipping away, falling out of your hands. Let them fall into the hands of God, who's always there to catch everything that needs to be caught – and let yourself release to him those things that you don't need to keep hold of. Feel the freedom, the lightness, as those concerns fall away.' *Pause . . . .*

3 Ask people to turn their hands over again so that the palms are facing upwards. 'Now your hands are open, but empty, no longer carrying the weights and burdens they were before, but ready now to receive all the good things God has to give you. God is always wanting to give us far more than we can imagine. Be open to receive whatever that is today, for yourself or for others. Be open . . . (*pause*).

4 The time of prayer can then proceed in whatever way the
leader wants.

5 At the end of the time of prayer, the leader may like to
bring the prayers back full circle by saying: 'Put your
hands back on your lap, palm upwards, and ask God to
give back to you those things you need to deal with, and
which he has kept safe. Some things you may find you
don't need to take back. Some things may come back
subtly changed – for God has been holding them. Be ready
to take your responsibilities, but always knowing that God
shares them with you, and that he holds you in the palm
of his hands . . . .'

(42) PRAYER TREE

The visual impact of a small, bare 'tree' can be considerable. Like a Christmas tree, it can be the bearer of our prayers, and the act of writing and hanging a prayer on the tree can be a satisfying way of participating in prayer for all ages.

What you need

1 The most difficult part of this form of prayer is finding a three- or four-foot section of tree branches that could look like a small tree when placed in a firm base. If a wander in the woods fails to turn up such a tree branch, then you might have to resort to a home-made variety or one drawn or painted on solid card.

2 Small pieces of card with string or cotton attached, enabling the card to be hung from a branch. If the string seems too much hassle to prepare, Blu-Tack® or equivalents can be used for the prayer cards instead.

3 Felt-tip pens.

What to do

1 Introduce the prayer tree as the focus for today's prayers. It might be used each week or just occasionally. You might refer to the image of 'the leaves of the tree (of life) are for the healing of the nations' in Revelation 22.2 – we are putting leaves on the tree as part of our cooperation with God in healing his world.

2 Everyone is given a card and felt pen and invited to write on it some of the things they would like to pray for. These could be related to the theme of the service or other guidance given. Assure people they don't need to write the

whole prayer down; just a word or phrase is enough. But be specific rather than general.

3 Then invite people to come up in their own time and hang their prayer card on the tree. Ask them to do it deliberately as an act of prayer, bringing the concern to God, rather than merely as a functional act. Quiet music could be played while this is happening.

4 When all have hung their cards, offer a gathering prayer, such as,

> Lord God our Father, we have brought to you some of our deep concerns and needs. We know you long to heal and save your people from everything that hurts and damages them. So take our prayers and use them to bless your world, for Jesus' sake.

5 Tell people the cards will stay there as a continuing form of prayer until next week (or whenever you think best).

Variations

If there are too many people for everyone to come up, the leader can invite people to come up as they come for communion or at the end of the service. If the tree is painted on card, the whole process can be done with stick-on notes.

(43) PRAYER BASKET

There's something satisfying about gathering prayers together in a symbolic way. It encourages variety and participation, and also represents the enfolding by God of our prayers and, indeed, our lives. One effective symbolic form is the basket. Prayers are placed into the basket as a way of bringing them into the embrace of God.

What you need

1   A substantial basket, ideally a wicker one, to be placed centrally and visibly but accessibly, so items can be placed in it without undue difficulty.

2   A variety of objects that sum up and represent the situations and people we're going to pray for.

3   People primed to bring up the symbolic items.

What to do

1   Decide what is to be prayed for and what items will adequately represent them: for example, a newspaper for this week's news, a map of the area for the needs of the community, a parish magazine for the life of the church or a poster for a particular event coming up, a candle for those who are ill, a Bible for the educational groups in church, a picture of the school or a school tie, and so on. The ideas are limitless.

2   Have these items at the back of the church or in the hands of particular people, ready to be brought up at the appropriate time.

3   The leading of the prayer can be done in two ways:

   (a) By informal commentary as the objects are brought up and placed in the basket followed by a time for silent prayer and a final 'Lord, hear us,' 'Lord, graciously hear us.'

(b) By formal words prepared in advance and said either by the leader or by the person bringing the object up. Again a time for silent prayer can be offered and a response given.

4 A final gathering-up prayer might be given by the leader.

5 This style of prayer works particularly well when there is a special focus to the service. For example, it can be useful in a school, where various symbols of its life can be brought up – a white-board marker pen, a school register, a kitchen implement, a school badge, a governors' meeting agenda, sports shoes, and so on. Each item can be brought up by someone representing that part of the school's life.

Variation

In a small group setting, members can be primed in advance to bring an object for which they are very thankful or which represents a need. One such occasion yielded a wedding ring, a dog's lead, a manuscript and a dish-cloth!

(44) SAND AND WATER

The basic elements of earth, wind, fire and water always seem to strike a chord when used in prayer. The following intercession uses two elements which echo common experiences on our spiritual journey. The size of the congregation or group will affect how the prayer is handled but with imagination this can be a moving time of prayer.

What you need

1   A tray or other receptacle containing soft sand, set on a table.

2   A jug of water with sufficient glasses for the size of the group, set on a separate table, or the other end of the same table.

3   Laminated prayers alongside these items, or prayers (below) on the service sheet.

What to do

1   Remind the congregation or group of the importance of the desert in the Bible – a place of *encounter with God* for Moses and the children of Israel and for Jesus as he went out to think through the nature of his task. It was also the place many early Christians went to discover themselves before God. Each of us has need of desert space in our lives where we can strip away the layers of protection and defence and meet God in silence and in love. Biblical passages could be read out (1 Kings 19.4–9; Matthew 4.1–11).

2   Remind the congregation or group that the desert is also *an image of dryness* often used in the psalms to express our need of God, for example: Psalm 63 'O God, you are my

101

God, earnestly I seek you, my soul thirsts for you; my flesh faints for you, as in a dry and weary land where there is no water.' We often experience that same need of God's refreshment. Biblical passages could be read out (Psalm 42.1–2; John 4.13–14).

3 Invite people to come out and do one of two things – or both. They could take a handful of sand and put it in their pocket (!) as a reminder of their need of a desert space in the rush of the week ahead. Or they could take a drink of water as a sign of their drawing on God's refreshing presence.

4 In a smallish group the words of the following prayers could be laid out on laminated cards alongside the sand and water. In a larger group or small congregation the prayers could be printed on cards or sheets given to each person beforehand. Each person would be invited to use that prayer either when they were enacting the symbolic action (small group) or when they had regained their seat (larger group).

5 When all are finished, the leader could pray a summative prayer.

Sample prayers by the sand and water

Sand: Lord, my life is often too full and too rushed to have space for you. May this sand be a reminder of the desert I need to find in my heart so that I can spend time with you. And may that time in the desert strengthen me to follow you, gently and confidently, in the ongoing rush of life. For Jesus' sake.

Water: Lord, I often feel spiritually dry and thirsty. May this water I have drunk be a reminder of the refreshment you constantly offer. May your Spirit restore me and enable me to find you, and to serve you in the thirsty lives of others. For Jesus' sake.

(45) BITTER AND SWEET

Like the prayer with sand and water, this form of prayer invites us to identify with one or other (or both) of the bitter or sweet experiences life brings us. The use of the sense of taste is a vivid reinforcement of the experience and adds vibrancy to our prayer. Be imaginative in the tastes you use!

What you need

1 A jar of honey that Winnie the Pooh would be proud of! And a plate of bread sticks. All this on a table.

2 A jar of a bitter food, or a dip with a sharp taste, or a bowlful of salt, again with bread sticks alongside, on a separate table, or the other end of the same table.

3 Depending on the size of the group, either two large laminated prayers alongside the honey and bitter food (small group), or a service sheet with the prayers printed out (larger group).

What to do

1 Explain that our experiences of life tend in the direction of being either sweet or bitter. Even this last week we will have had a number of experiences which fit into either category. Some of them will have been particularly good or particularly bad, and it's about those that we're going to pray. Suggest some of the sweet or bitter things that may be around.

2 Invite people to think quietly about which experiences they're especially aware of this week. They may be things to do with themselves, or their family and friends, or things in the news. The important thing is that they are, to a degree, on our hearts and therefore something to share with God.

3 Then invite people to come up in their own time and go to one or other (or both) of the tables and there to dip a bread stick in the honey or the bitter food, and taste it, while saying the prayer on the laminated card (small group) or reflecting on the situation prior to going back to their seat and saying the prayer on the service sheet (larger group).

4 When all are finished, the leader can offer a summing-up prayer.

Sample prayers by the honey and the bitter food

Honey: Lord, I'm so grateful for this experience this week. Thank you for the effect it had on me (and on others). Help me to retain the memory and the thankfulness, and let them be in me an inspiration to a life of deeper praise and service of others. For Jesus' sake.

Bitter food: Lord, I'm feeling the pain of this situation (as are others). I pray that the light of your presence in this darkness will give me a clue about how to start building back towards the goodness that you want for us all. In the meantime, keep me on track, for Jesus' sake.

(46) TO THE CROSS

One understanding of intercessory prayer is that it's a way of bringing people to the cross, where Christ is sure to be found. And where Christ is found, things happen. The cross can be used in many ways as the focus of our prayers, particularly in Holy Week.

What you need

1   A large wooden cross, such as many churches have for Holy Week, set up in front of the congregation or group.

2   Removable self-stick notes or small pieces of paper with Blu-Tack®.

3   Pens or pencils.

What to do

1   Explain about prayer being a matter of bringing ourselves, our needs and the needs of others to the cross where Christ meets us and deals with whatever we bring him.

2   Give out self-stick notes and pens, and invite people to write or draw their prayer to take to the cross. Explain that the prayer can be about something that links with the theme of the service, or a concern, a person in need, something to confess, or whatever is on people's hearts. Give some examples. Say that drawing may be easier for some because it avoids naming specific people or situations.

3   Give people time to write, perhaps playing quiet music in the background.

4   Invite people to come up in their own time and stick their note to the cross, and to do that prayerfully and

105

deliberately, not just in a perfunctory way. The music can still be playing.

5 At the end, the leader can say a prayer which gathers up all the prayers offered, or all can sing a hymn of the passion, such as 'When I survey the wondrous cross.'

Variations

The method can be used to focus one particular form of prayer, such as confession. Prayer notes can then be brought up and given to a designated person who deliberately hammers each note to the cross to emphasize that 'we believe it was for us he hung and suffered there'. The cross needs to be well supported to withstand the hammering – as may do our emotions! Alternatively, the cross can be laid flat, as was Jesus' cross when he was put onto it.

(47) SPARKLERS

There's something captivating about sparklers, as captivating as we hope prayer might be. Using sparklers can add zest and life to a time of prayer, but adequate precautions should be taken! It's possible to buy 'indoor' sparklers, although they might seem a bit tame in a large building. We need to remember not only the danger of any form of firework but also the fact that some children (and adults) are quite fearful of them.

What you need

1 A number of sparklers, of indoor or outdoor variety.

2 Either good, strong matches, or a candle with a sufficiently powerful flame to light the sparklers. It's embarrassing if the sparklers won't light!

What to do

1 Explain to the group or congregation that prayer is a many-splendoured activity and can be offered in all sorts of ways. The way we're going to use now is one where we pray with our eyes open and keep a particular period of time for our own silent prayer. The way we're going to pray is with sparklers, and the time it takes for the sparkler to run its course is the time we'll take to pray about each special need.

2 Think aloud about the kind of things we might all want to pray about today – things in the news, people with particular needs, events coming up, things to celebrate. Then ask for items for prayer.

3 As a prayer request is named ask that person whether they will come out and hold their 'prayer sparkler'. Have someone primed to come and help out if they'd rather not.

Then light the sparkler from match or candle, have it held high, and ask people to pray quietly for that need for as long as the sparkler is active.

4 Repeat as often as you have time or feel it is being helpful.

5 At the end you may want to light a final candle yourself and gather up all sorts of other needs you know people have, or balance out 'domestic' prayers with wider concerns. Your final prayer might include the request that our light may so shine before others this week that they are drawn to Jesus Christ, who is the Light of the world, and gives sparkle to all of life.

(48) PRAYING THE WEEK'S NEWS

These intercessions are for two voices, alternating between extracts from the week's newspapers and prayerful responses to those items of news. The attempt is to hold together the real world in which people live and work, and the infinite resources of the God whose world it actually is. As such it is just one way of keeping up the pressure to stop us domesticating God within the confines of the church.

VOICE 1 *reads a paragraph of good news from a newspaper.*

VOICE 2 Father, thank you for that. We don't often notice the good news. Make us more aware of successes, generous acts, people celebrating, outbreaks of peace and, in our own experience, the steady procession of good things through our lives.

Lord, in your mercy, **hear our prayer.**

VOICE 1 *reads a paragraph of bad news from home or abroad.*

VOICE 2 Father, that news hurts. Or it should. Too easily it becomes sad but ordinary, as more and more news pours across our vision. Save us from trivializing the suffering of people like those in that piece of news. Indeed, we pray for them now, that your good and gracious presence may give them what they need in these dark days.

Lord, in your mercy, **hear our prayer.**

VOICE 1 *reads a paragraph of news that affects the Church.*

VOICE 2 Father, that issue is our issue because we are the Church. Save us from blaming others, 'them', the bishops, 'the

Church', when those others are really 'us'. Give us confidence in our mandate from you. Help us to speak with passion and clarity about issues that affect the social and spiritual health of the nation. And give us courage in proclaiming that Jesus Christ is Lord.

Lord, in your mercy, **hear our prayer.**

Voice 1 *reads a paragraph about someone's illness or death.*

Voice 2 Father, that illness/death made the newspapers. Behind it is a depth of sorrow that we know little of. And so it is behind every story and every name, when someone is ill or bereaved: most of us know nothing. But every story and every name is known and precious to you. We bring to you, therefore, our own people in need on this day, and name them in silence or out loud for you to bless them and hold them close . . . .

Lord, in your mercy, **hear our prayer.**

Voice 1 Father, we are bombarded with so much news. Make us discerning and prayerful listeners to the news this coming week. And make us ready to bring good news to the poor, release to the captives, recovery of sight to the blind, and to proclaim your loving presence in the heart of every event in every week, through Jesus Christ, our living Lord. Amen.

(49) PURPLE RIBBON

*I first used this way of praying at a wedding (my daughter's!).
However, the method is applicable in other contexts too: for any
group of people making a commitment, a confirmation group,
people preparing for some form of authorized ministry, and so
on. The value is in the symbolic action of tying the ribbon and in
the keeping of the ribbon afterwards as a reminder of the
commitment and the need for continuing prayer.*

What you need

Sufficient pieces of ribbon (it doesn't need to be purple), cut to
25–30 cms length, and given out either before the worship event
or at the time of prayer.

What to do (a full text)

1 For our prayers today we're going to use the purple ribbon
   you had in your order of service. And I want to give us
   sufficient time to really pray for A and B, not just to listen
   to a prayer said by someone else.

2 So would you take the ribbon and simply tie a knot in the
   middle. The two ends join – A and B, coming together,
   'tying the knot' (as they say). They've committed their
   whole lives to each other, in that wonderful, wild,
   dangerous activity we call marriage. And all heaven
   celebrates with them.

   So as you look at, or hold, that knot you've just tied,
   would you, in a time of silent prayer, give thanks for this
   great moment – and pray God's blessing on, around and
   within A and B's marriage? . . .

      Circle, Lord, your servants A and B with your
         inexhaustible love . . . .

111

3 Now please take one end of the ribbon and tie another knot. Let that knot represent the many others who've married recently – maybe some here? – or let it represent your own marriage or special relationship.

And in silence again, as you look at or hold that knot, please pray for those others or for yourselves, praying for grace or trust or joy or forgiveness or whatever is most important in that relationship. Let's pray now . . . .

Circle, Lord, these couples for whom we pray, with your protecting presence . . . .

4 Now please take the other end of the ribbon and tie a third knot. As you do that, remember those whose relationships have ended up in the wrong kind of knot – one that seems like a tangle, a mess. And other kinds of relationships – political, international, social – knots that seem implacable, utterly resistant to reason and change. Name these knots – people and situations – in your heart, and in silence, pray for them . . . .

Circle, Lord, these people and these places with your healing grace . . . .

5 God of love, as you have brought A and B together in mutual offering, so deepen their love for each other and their love for you, that they may find in their marriage kindness and gentleness, joy and celebration, renewal and hope – for in you is their life, shaped around Jesus Christ our Lord.

(50) INCENSE

*Why should this splendid aid to prayer only be used by one
tradition in the Church? The idea of prayer rising like incense and
leaving an aroma of sanctity is deeply rooted in Jewish practice in
the Old Testament and is an image used by St Paul of the lives of
Christians. The sight and the aroma of incense gives strong
sensual reinforcement to our prayers, although we need to
remember that some people have a strong physical reaction to
incense and it may be too powerful to use in a confined space.*

What you need

1   The most difficult part is finding an appropriate steel bowl
    for the charcoal. It needs to be about mixing-bowl size,
    without a lid, and capable of standing on a table or stool in
    view of the group or congregation.

2   Charcoal and incense from a specialist shop (ecclesiastical
    or other). The charcoal is put in the mixing bowl, and
    incense in another small bowl, with a teaspoon alongside.

3   Matches.

What to do

1   Explain that we are going to pray by putting grains of
    incense on glowing charcoal and letting our prayers be
    taken to God. Explain also, and briefly, the Old Testament
    and New Testament background of incense in worship
    (Psalm 141.2; 2 Corinthians 2.14–16).

2   Light the charcoal. Illustrate how to take a small spoonful
    of incense and drop it on the charcoal, and see the effect.

3   Invite people to pray. They come up and put a little incense
    on the charcoal, using the spoon. In a small group people
    may want to say what they are praying for and invite our

113

participation. In a larger group or congregation, the action itself may be sufficient; God knows the content of our prayers.

4 Draw the prayers together with your own prayer at the end. For example,

> Father in heaven, you delight to receive the prayers of your people, and even more, you delight to answer them. Receive these our prayers which we have released to you, and let their fragrance fill the halls of heaven, through Jesus Christ our Lord.

4 INTERCESSIONS WITH CHILDREN AND YOUNG PEOPLE

PRACTICALITIES

This is a checklist of principles to bear in mind when preparing intercessions for children and young people.

1   Participation has to be carefully judged. Different groups will respond in different ways and we need to go with the developing life and practice of the group rather than expect it to be what it isn't. The older children get, of course, the greater the probability of embarrassment. And nothing is worse than that for many a teenager. Don't push it!

2   A 'centring' phase is nearly always necessary. It's hard for younger people to drop their engagement with another activity and suddenly to focus on prayer. We need to allow time to adjust to this new activity, through music, lighting a candle, sitting still, and generally calming down and centring.

3   If you hit a winner, stay with it! You never know which form of prayer will catch young people's imagination and which will leave them cold. If you find a method that really helps them to pray, repeat it and develop it.

4   Conversely, if a method fails, drop it! You may be inclined to think that a particular way into prayer is brilliant and be determined to persist with it until the group sees how wonderful it is. In this case, the customer is always right!

5   Age and method are crucially linked. Again, we can very easily fail to realize that a particular form of praying is associated in the group's mind with a younger age-group. Children's and teenagers' habits are very age-specific.

6   **Encourage children's imagination.** Children are very often far more receptive to spirituality than we realize, and far more imaginative in their responses and perceptions. Their comments and questions can very often be stunning to the jaded adult imagination! We need to encourage, listen, affirm and build on what we are given in their responses. As they get older, children will usually become more private and capable of embarrassment. Be sensitive!

7   **Preparation time increases in proportion to the creativity of the idea.** Never skimp in terms of the time taken to prepare, think through and experiment with a new idea for intercession or any other form of prayer.

8   **Be prepared for times of total failure and times of pure magic!**

(51) RITUALS

Most of us value ritual more than we realize and children are usually too young to be self-conscious about it! Using an appropriate ritual can become a very valuable way of entering or introducing a time of prayer. Watch for the point at which the ritual has outlived its usefulness, and beware the ritual that appeals to you but not to the young people!

Lighting a candle

This is the most basic and familiar ritual to use in praying with children or young people. The lighting of the candle – preferably by a child – marks the time set apart for prayer. It can be accompanied by suitable words. For example:

Jesus said, 'I am the light of the world. Whoever follows me will not walk in darkness but will have the light of life.' (John 8.12)

The light shines in the darkness, and the darkness has never put it out. (John 1.5)

Shine, Jesus, shine; fill this land with the Father's glory.

'Signature tune' music

It can be helpful to have a piece of music played on CD which everyone knows announces the time for prayer. The choice of music is of course entirely particular and personal to the group. It may be some form of Praise Guitar, or a Taizé chant, or a piece of classical music or a contemporary song, but the same music needs to be used for some considerable time to establish its identity as a signal for prayer.

A 'prayer bag'

This can be useful with smaller children. Have a recognizable bag
out of which you draw different items which lead into a
particular type of prayer: for example, a bottle of water, a pair of
glasses, a football, a newspaper, a computer game (the
associations are yours!). As this bag emerges each week, there is a
sense of expectation and inquisitiveness which develops in the
children, and their attention is caught.

(52) HAZELNUTS

Natural objects have an immediate and obvious appeal. The great doorway they can open for prayer is that of wonder. Once wonder is aroused it can easily lead into intercession. Hazelnuts are reasonably easy to obtain and they link well with Julian of Norwich's famous observation below.

What you need

1   Simply a bowl full of hazelnuts.

2   With an older group you may like to have the words of Julian of Norwich as well. Julian of Norwich was a fourteenth-century hermit who had a remarkable series of visions on which she pondered for years before writing the *Revelations of Divine Love*, from which comes the following quote:

> God showed me in my palm a little thing round as a ball about the size of a hazelnut. I looked at it with the eye of my understanding and asked myself: 'What is this thing?' And I was answered: 'It is everything that is created.' I wondered how it could survive since it seemed so little it could suddenly disintegrate into nothing. The answer came: 'It endures, and ever will endure, because God loves it.' And so everything has its being because of God's love.

What to do

1   Each person takes a hazelnut from a bowl as it's passed round the group. The leader raises a series of questions about the hazelnuts: How come this fragile little thing exists? Isn't it incredible that there isn't any hazelnut anywhere in creation that's exactly like the one you're holding now? How does this hazelnut manage to continue

to exist? Depending on the group, you may get answers to your questions or the questions may be rhetorical.

2 The answer to each of these questions, according to Julian of Norwich, is because God loves it – plain and simple. And profound. Nothing would exist without the sustaining power and love of God.

3 This can then lead into prayer as gratitude and wonder. Suggestions can come from the group as to what strikes them as astonishing or beautiful or 'awesome', and each of these has the potential, if appropriate, to be turned into intercession as well. For example, wonder at the pattern of clouds that day can lead into prayer for the environment because of our changing weather patterns as a result of global warming. Or wonder at the variety of flowers in our gardens can lead to prayer for gardeners and those who try to make our parks and public spaces beautiful.

4 Let the group take their hazelnuts home as a reminder of their own uniqueness, and of the prayers they have shared.

(53) MAPS AND GLOBES

An effective way of praying with a map of the world is outlined in The Intercessions Handbook, p. 147. *Because it works well, I refer to it again here, but with significant variations. It seems to be a method of praying for the world which engages people's attention and imagination.*

The basic idea

Have a wall map laid out on the floor or a table, some night-lights arranged around the edge of the map, a large white candle and a taper. Light the big candle while repeating the words of Jesus: 'I am the light of the world.' 'The light shines in the darkness and the darkness has never put it out.' Then invite people to come forward and light one of the night-lights from the large candle, and place it somewhere on the map where there is special need (war, famine, unrest, torture), or where they have a special contact (family, friend, mission partner). Then they can pray out loud or keep a silence for all to pray, ending with 'Lord in your mercy,' 'hear our prayer.' Repeat as often as is helpful, then 'fill in the gaps' and gather all the intercessions together in a concluding prayer.

Variation 1 – a single region

Focus on one country or continent and, by question and answer, draw out the different aspects of that country which we could be praying for. This prevents the praying being too superficial ('God bless India'), and allows the method to be a regular part of the educational and praying programme of the group. You could draw out the many needs of India – reliable harvests to feed her fast-growing population, settlements with neighbours of dangerous border disputes, greater tolerance for the Christian Church, proper human rights for the 'untouchables'. A little research by the leader will make this time of prayer more challenging and helpful.

Variation 2 – 'takeaway' prayer

Members of the group could be given a small card with 'their' country on it – either the country they have prayed for or another that the leader gives out. They could be asked to do two things during the week: (1) Continue to pray for that place; (2) Listen out for any mention of the country during the week, in the news or at school, or they could try and find out more about the country (on the internet?) to feed back to the group the next week. So the praying is enriched.

Variation 3 – a globe, and outstretched hands

A globe could be used instead of a map. Either the leader or the members of the group could try and find the places they would like to pray for. As above, some of the facts and needs of the country could be drawn out, and then the children or young people could be asked to stretch out a hand towards the globe in blessing, as the leader says a prayer. This gives greater ownership of the prayer by each person.

(54) PEBBLES IN WATER

Water has an elemental quality which readily attracts and engages us. It's often best when in movement – flowing, bubbling, raging – but it can also be a metaphor for stillness, restoration and enveloping. Here we use these latter ideas in an activity which can speak to people of any age.

What you need

1   A strong glass bowl full of clear water.

2   An appropriate number of medium-sized stones collected from the seashore or bought from a well-known Scandinavian furniture store!

What to do

1   Explain that when we pray it's like putting our prayer into the enormous ocean of God's love. More specifically it's like putting the person we're praying for into that huge sea, and letting God take and embrace that person to give them what they most deeply need. Through our prayer, that person is soaked in God's love.

2   Explain that we're going to think about who or what we want to pray for, and then we're going to take a pebble, if we want to, and let it be our prayer, and then place it gently into the bowl, saying who it's for as we do so.

3   Demonstrate with a prayer for someone or some situation all the group knows. Place the stone carefully in the water, saying, 'This is my prayer for X, who needs this prayer because . . . .' Then say a simple responsory, such as, 'Lord, in your mercy,' 'hear our prayer.'

4   Then have a short time of silence while people decide who or what they are going to pray for, and then invite them to

123

start (with a little gentle encouragement if necessary!). Ask them not to rush but truly to pray as they place the pebbles in the water.

5 End with a gathering-up prayer such as:

Lord God, you know the people we have prayed for and you love them even more than we do. Take our prayers and use them for good purposes. Let these prayers be like acts of love rippling out to all the world, making this a better place for everyone. Through Jesus Christ our Lord. Amen.

(55) PLAYING CARDS

Using familiar objects in a different setting can be a helpful way of engaging the imagination of people – young and old – for prayer. Playing cards are useful, although, as ever, they must serve the purpose of true prayer and not simply be a gimmick. This is usually achieved through the sincerity of the leader of the prayers.

What you need

Simply a pack of cards. Remove the jokers. Shuffle the pack.

What to do

1 Explain that the four suits of cards can have many different meanings. You are simply choosing a particular set of meanings to enable us to pray today.

2 Put the cards face down on a table and turn over the top one. The following is an imaginary order – it doesn't matter how they emerge.

3 *Hearts*: 'With this card we're going to pray for people who are special to us, who have our heart.' Either draw out from the group who those people are, or give them space to think of such people for themselves. Then pray a collective prayer of thanks for all these people, being careful to remember that for some young people their home experience may be ambivalent.

4 *Spades*: 'With this card we're going to pray for working people who put in a lot of effort for others – be it their family or society as a whole.' Draw out from the group who they'd like to pray for. This is an opportunity to bring out the more unusual professions and jobs. We're used to praying for teachers and medics in intercessions, but not so used to praying for call-centre workers, labourers on

building sites, financial services advisers, pilots and air crew, etc. Try not to be too generalized in your collective prayer – think what the particular needs of each working group might be.

5 *Clubs*: 'With this card we pray for people caught up in war, terrorism, violent crime and domestic violence.' The news will (sadly) provide many current examples of people and situations to pray for. Make sure your prayer isn't too depressing! Pray for peace-keepers, the police, and the good will, eyes and ears of ordinary people looking after each other.

6 *Diamonds*: 'With this card we pray for the many people in our world who need more good things – not usually diamonds!, but food, education, clean water, available medical care, etc.' Remember also that millions of families in Britain fall beneath the poverty line – draw attention to forgotten pockets of poverty nearby.

7 Pick up the cards and shuffle them again. 'We're all mixed up in the glorious jumble of God's people.' Hold out the pack. 'God loves us all, and he loves us to love each other. Lord, hold us in the palm of your hand, and keep us safe – together. Amen.'

(56) THE COMPASS AND THE MAGNET

When you're young and discovering life's glamorous temptations, it's very hard to keep a straight course. This intercession tries to do justice to that difficulty and to offer a vivid image to help young people focus on their choices.

What you need

1 An Ordnance Survey-type map, preferably of country terrain.

2 A functioning compass.

3 A magnet.

What to do

1 Explain that these prayers are about keeping on the right track when you're surrounded by many very attractive opportunities to wander into tricky places.

2 Lay out the map on a table and set the compass in the middle of the map. Gather the children/young people around the table. Demonstrate how the compass always turns to magnetic North. Talk about how living as a Christian is like trying to point our lives towards the 'magnetic North' of Jesus – to live our lives towards him. He gives us 'the way' to get to 'the truth', which in turn will give us 'the life' we really seek. Perhaps give thanks for Jesus as our goal and guide.

3 Ask for volunteers to say what pulls them or others (or people more generally) away from following the way of Jesus. Give the volunteer a magnet to move along the edge of the map and show how the needle of the compass follows the magnet. Lead an extempore prayer for all (of us) who get drawn away from Christ by that particular

attraction or temptation. This is not a time for prayer with closed eyes – watching the effect of the magnet is vital.

4 Repeat as often as there are volunteers. If they slow up, throw in a few problem areas of your own. Depending on the age of the group, these may be: problems with parents, anger that takes us over, jealousy of popular people in our class, delirious attraction to a particular boy/girl, etc.

5 Bring to a close by making clear that we never get away from these distractions that pull us off-centre. What matters is that we try to distance ourselves from the problem area either by removing ourselves from it or by removing the temptation. And when we fail – because we will – the Good News is that God never turns away from us but welcomes us back on track. Final prayer of thanks for such a gracious and broad-minded God!

(57) STONES HAVE SHARP EDGES

*Stones can symbolize many things. One of them is their hardness
and their tendency sometimes to have sharp edges. What follows
is a way of prayer for young people more than for children,
allowing them to address some of the negatives they find within
themselves and don't know how to handle.*

What you need

1 Stones picked up from the garden or elsewhere and washed.
   The stones need to have some sharp edges.

2 A bowl to contain the stones.

What to do

1 Pass a bowl of stones around the group and ask each
   member to take one. The leader talks them through the
   way this stone they now have in their hand can represent
   many things, including their uniqueness and strength, but
   also their tough experiences, or their 'sharp edges' that
   continually get them into trouble. 'What are those things in
   your life? How much of a mess do they lead you into?
   What have you done about those things to try and deal
   with them?'

2 Say that what you are offering members of the group is the
   opportunity to take the tough things in their lives to Christ
   on the cross. It may be their particular area of hardness of
   heart or their particular sharp edges, the things they're fed
   up with doing and the mistakes they make. They can
   simply take them to Jesus on the cross and leave them
   there. That's what Jesus came to do – to lighten our
   burdens, to deal with our bad stuff and to enable us to
   change.

3 Now ask members of the group to take their stones to the cross set before them (either in the centre of the group or beyond it) and, in their own time, lay their stone down at the foot of the cross, and so leave with Jesus that hard area of life. Background music, played softly, might help. Tell people not to rush, nor to feel compelled to do anything if they don't want to.

4 Bring this time of prayer to an end with your own concluding prayer, asking for God's grace and strength as we seek to live more closely to the potential God sees in us.

(58) PRAYER BUBBLES

There's something lastingly attractive about the delicate bubbles produced by blowing through the circular instrument in the little tubes of liquid you can easily buy from toy shops. The bubbles come out with a rush; some burst immediately; others drift slowly around, eventually finding their way into oblivion. Here is an obvious way in to prayer with children, or at an all-age service.

What you need

1   A tube (or two) of bubble liquid.

2   A sensible volunteer!

What to do

1   Say that prayer is a strong – but also a delicate – activity, sometimes offered tentatively because we can't know exactly how we ought to pray or for what. So the delicate bubbles from this prayer activity may seem appropriate for some of our prayers.

2   Ask for a volunteer child to blow the bubbles, choosing someone who can be relied on not to blow furiously or ineffectually. Ask the child to experiment with blowing bubbles first in order to be sure it's going to work when the time comes and also so that the watching children can simply delight in the bubbles for a moment. If possible, put the child in a safe place somewhat higher than everyone else so the bubbles will be seen and will have further to fall before they burst.

3   Explain that when you've gathered a few prayers you'll ask for some bubbles to be blown and then everyone will be able to pray about those things for as long as the bubbles are in the air. Then you'll gather a few more prayers and repeat.

4 Ask what the children would like to pray about – people, situations, events in their lives. If necessary (it probably won't be!) give a few examples to set them off. When you have two or three, recap simply what you're praying for and have the child blow some bubbles. While the bubbles remain in the air, floating gently towards the floor, they represent our prayers, and the children can focus their gaze on the beauty and delicacy of the prayer-bubbles.

5 Repeat.

6 Concluding prayer. For example,

> God of beauty and love, you have heard our prayers as we watched the bubbles descend to the ground. Thank you for the lightness, colour and delicacy of those bubbles and for the things we've thought about as we watched them. Please take everything we've asked for and thought about, and give us the answers that are best for everyone. For Jesus' sake.

(59) MUSIC AND DVD/VIDEO

If we are hoping to show that prayer is related to the real-life experience of young people then we have to recognize the pervasive influence of music and films. There are obviously a number of extra factors here for leaders. (1) Finding what music is current, not 'naff', and available, is time-consuming. It's easy to miss young people's real interests by a month, a faux-pas, *or a nuance of the youth culture! So we need to use their tastes and knowledge. (2) It could seem gimmicky to the young people themselves and not be particularly prayerful. Having recognized all that, this is a powerful medium, and why should prayer not use the best opportunities it has?*

Ideas

1   A top-selling CD of the moment might have songs with very interesting lyrics (if you can make them out). The young people themselves are the best source of interesting music. At the appropriate time, a song can be introduced, played and then discussed before leading into prayer about the issues raised. Who can they think of who might be affected by these issues at the moment?

2   Play a section from a popular film out on DVD/video which raises issues to do with trust, loyalty, friendship, temptation, fear, peer pressure and so on. Many films could be recommended, but clearly *The Lord of the Rings* trilogy and the *Harry Potter* films will be useable for some time and relate to many of the themes above. There are cameo moments in almost every film these days – *Bridget Jones's Diary, Four Weddings and a Funeral*, and *Love, Actually* all use humour as a good way into serious issues about relationships. Films like *The Shawshank Redemption, The Green Mile, Dead Poets Society*, and *Rain Man* are all suitable too. Discussion of these films would need to lead

to a consideration of who in the knowledge of the group or in society generally might be in need of God's supporting, protecting or guiding presence.

3 If you are quite creative and have the time, a combination of music and film can be highly effective. For example, using the *Jesus of Nazareth* video scene of the crucifixion (without the sound) with the Bryan Adams' song 'Everything I do (I do it for you)' is a very moving meditation. Timing of music and film clip is crucial. Don't use the Mel Gibson film *The Passion of the Christ*, which is too raw and brutal.

(60) PRAYER ZONE

There could be an occasion when a major effort could be made with a children's or youth group on prayer. You could then establish a complete part of the church (a side chapel?) or a large room or small hall as a Prayer Zone. This could have in it a range of different opportunities for prayer and activities to catch the imagination of the group. They could then be given different times during the week when the Prayer Zone will be available, and they could come and go when they wanted. They might well come back with their parents, and the rest of the congregation would probably be asking for their turn too!

Here are some of the things that could go in the Prayer Zone, all with the very important instruction: Take time, don't rush.

– **Background music,** such as a Taizé CD, Praise Guitar, one of the many 'mood music' CDs now available (from Christian bookshops).

– **A mirror,** beside which are guidelines about looking in the mirror and remembering that we are made in the image of God and are unique. Don't look and despair; look and be amazed at what you can do and at the love which fashioned you so brilliantly. Psalm 139.1–18 should be available in large print and as a takeaway.

– **Many night lights** laid out in the shape of a cross with an invitation to light a candle for each prayer offered or each person prayed for. Or the night lights could be in a pile and people be invited to make their own configurations and to light them while they pray. Leave the candles burning (within the limits of safety!). Takeaway card: 'Ask and it will be given you, search and you will find, knock and the door will be opened for you' (Luke 11.9).

- **A vase,** with various flowers (dried or otherwise), bits of greenery, etc. in a bucket alongside. An invitation to think of things you are really grateful for and to place a flower in the vase for each act of thanksgiving. What gets built up is something beautiful for God, an offering to him as an act of thanksgiving.

- **Dart board** – without darts! Stick-on notes alongside with the invitation to put some personal code on the note representing a failure, sin, mess, etc. The note is then placed somewhere on the board, at a position representing how we think we 'missed the mark'. Maybe a takeaway card with the quote: 'Neither do I condemn you. Go, and do not sin again' (John 8.11).

- **A pile of stones,** and a cross. An invitation to choose a stone as a symbol of some hard place in the young person's life – a relationship, school work, a private despair – and to place that stone carefully at the foot of the cross. Maybe a takeaway card with the verse, 'Come to me, all you who are weary and are carrying heavy burdens, and I will give you rest' (Matthew 11.28).

- **Sand tray,** with the invitation to smooth the sand out and then make a footprint or handprint. The accompanying words ask the reader to think who has been for them someone to follow, whose footprint they have tried to walk in or whose hand has helped them on their way. Give thanks for that person and resolve to be an example to others.

- **Books.** Depending on the age of the group, there could be part of the Zone with books, magazines, articles, DIY activities all around the theme of prayer. Big cushions would be useful here.

- **A large icon** or a large poster of the Taizé cross, with a big candle alongside, and one or two prayer stools, for those who would like the opportunity to just 'be'. Maybe some guidelines on how to be still before God. Takeaway card: 'Be still, and know that I am God' (Psalm 46.10).

- **An area with paper,** ball-points, coloured pens, etc. for people either to write (a letter to God? a response to something they've done elsewhere in the room? a poem?), or to create a larger visual 'painting' as a form of prayer or response to the room.

- **A world map,** as described elsewhere in this section, with night lights for people to place their prayers on the countries in need of the light of Christ. Takeaway: 'The light shines in the darkness, and the darkness has never overcome it' (John 1.5).

- **Bread and wine.** With older groups there could be bread and wine, a pottery chalice and plate, with a candle alongside and a copy of the communion service, and a book giving a parallel commentary on what goes on and why. Sit and read/think/pray. Takeaway could be the words of institution from 1 Corinthians 11.23–6.

- **Graffiti board.** An opportunity to write any reflection which has come out of using the room – a thought, a prayer, an idea. Anything decent and honest!

The ideas can keep on coming. The important points are:

- to make the content applicable to the age, stage and type of groups who will use the Prayer Zone;

- to emphasize the rule: Don't rush, take time;

- to make sure that the instructions are clear;

- to make sure the presentation of each part of the Zone is attractive;

- to clean up the Zone after each session of use.

Then let the Lord the Spirit do the rest!

AND ALSO . . .

These are just seed ideas which can be developed in different ways.

(61) . . . JIGSAWS

It's possible to cut a large piece of card into jigsaw-type shapes (maybe six or eight pieces) with a clear middle piece that holds the others together. You then ask the group what they want to pray for out of the week past, or their session just now, and start placing the pieces together, offering a prayer each time – silent or spoken. The central piece can go in first or last but it represents Jesus Christ, the one through whom we pray. Either our prayers take shape around him, or he comes in last to hold our prayers together and take them to the Father.

(62) . . . NEWSPAPER PHOTOGRAPHS

You bring a number of pictures from the week's newspapers, showing events, people, violence, sports, etc. You then work with the group deciding how you can pray about these situations. (How do you pray about sports events, even though they're so important in people's lives?) Deep engagement will probably come out of these discussions, and you can then pray over each photo, commending the situation or person to God. Not only are you praying but you're also teaching others how to pray (and learning yourself!).

(63) . . . CANDLES

You can't go far wrong with candles! They might be night lights, or short candles to stick into a sand tray, or candles in a holder to be hand held. They can be arranged beforehand in the shape of a cross to be lit as prayers are offered, or arranged in a circle so the end result is a pool of light, or a single candle handed on to the next person so they can be prayed for silently or aloud. They can be lit at the start of the prayer time, or placed on a map of your town, or carried round a darkened church in procession. The permutations are endless!

(64) . . . GODLY PLAY

This is a way of telling biblical stories very carefully, using figures and artefacts to build up the story and carry the different stages of the narrative. It has a growing literature (see the Resources section at the end of the book) and a fast-growing following. Children of all ages are usually captivated and the atmosphere at the end of a story is usually very conducive to a short, meditative prayer.

(65) . . . P.U.S.H.

These letters stand for Pray Until Something Happens! Simple bracelets, pens and many other things can be bought with this acronym on it, or with a little effort can be home-made. A prayer card with PUSH! on it can be given to every member of the group. You can then set the challenge to the group to pray until something happens for a common need or for personal issues. Beware false expectations but not true expectancy! Here is a good opportunity to teach and think together about what prayer is and how God uses our prayers.

5 INTERCESSIONS IN PERSONAL PRAYER

PRACTICALITIES

This is a checklist of principles to bear in mind when working out how best to intercede in your personal prayer:

1   Adopt practices that are liberating and not guilt-inducing. Find ways that encourage you and don't make you feel more guilty about your intercession. Most of us carry enough guilt around with us without another load from our prayers!

2   Recognize the importance of the physical setting of prayer. We pray best when we are comfortable with our bodies and with our surroundings. This means finding a place, a time and a selection of artefacts – cross, candle, icon, prayer stool, CD player, stones, Bible, books of poems, etc. To have a regular place means that we drop more quickly into prayer, surrounded by things of proven usefulness.

3   Take account of the relationship between personality and prayer. This is now a well-established link and can be a very liberating discovery for those who have always felt that what they were told about prayer didn't work for them. The Myers Briggs Personality Type Indicator has helped many to identify where their spiritual home is, thus freeing them to go on spiritual journeys and bring back treasures from 'abroad', while feeling secure in their own spiritual identity.

4   Recognize that discipline is an essential part of any life of prayer. No serious engagement with prayer is possible without some struggle with boredom, dryness, dull duty and frustration.

Discipline is as essential to prayer as it is to training at sport or learning computer skills. But discipline is the doorway to freedom.

5   Every so often, examine how satisfactory your way of intercession seems to be. See if it's got into a rut. Be prepared to try other approaches to retain or regain the urgency and liveliness of intercession.

6   Be prepared to review what God has done in the situations you have been praying about. This may feel either scary or distrustful, but it's actually a lovely opportunity to see and wonder at how God has been at work in unexpected ways. And that's really encouraging!

7   Consider sharing your intercession with others as well as being your own. This stops your intercession being a private possession, comfortable and 'neat'. Perhaps you can join another person for a prayer partnership, or join a prayer group. Perhaps you can ask others to pray for a particular need, and ask also for their reflections on the situation you've been praying for. Or you might find a 'spiritual director'/companion to talk over your prayer and intercession with. All of this may result in you praying in slightly different ways, being opened up to surprises.

8   Intercession must be kept in balance with other forms of prayer. Intercession is only one form of prayer. Prayer is getting hold of God before it's getting hold of 'answers'. So we are drawn to thanksgiving, confession, wonder, desperation and silent resting, as well as to intercession. Sometimes, in fact, intercession can be an easy way of avoiding direct contact with the living God; it may be easier to run through a list of needs than to face the searching gaze of Love. A healthy balance is needed, usually with intercession following on from the re-establishing of our intimate relationship with God in thanksgiving and honest self-examination.

(66) PREPARATION:
ST PATRICK'S BREASTPLATE

The famous prayer popularly known as St Patrick's Breastplate can be a helpful preparation for any time of personal prayer because it places us securely within the light and protection of Christ.

If it is your practice to light a candle to mark out your time of prayer then using this prayer can be the next thing you do. It should be said unhurriedly. *Christ be with me . . . Christ within me . . . .* It should be said thoughtfully. *Christ behind me . . . Christ before me . . . .* It can also be said visually, i.e. we can imagine the protective presence of Christ around us. *Christ beside me . . . Christ to win me . . . .* It should also be said heart to heart. *Christ to comfort and restore me . . . .*

The prayer reminds us that nothing is outside the reach of Christ. *Christ beneath me, Christ above me . . . .* Best of all, the prayer is short and simple enough to be learnt and is therefore available to us at any time when we need the reassurance of Christ's presence. *Christ in quiet . . . Christ in danger . . . .* It includes a prayer for our family and special friends. *Christ in hearts of all who love me . . . .* It also encourages us to look for Christ throughout the day. *Christ in mouth of friend and stranger . . . .*

Whenever the prayer is used, but particularly at the start of the day, there comes with it a galvanizing confidence that we are secure in the armour of God, the presence of Christ.

Christ be with me, Christ within me
Christ behind me, Christ before me
Christ beside me, Christ to win me
Christ to comfort and restore me

Christ beneath me, Christ above me
Christ in quiet, Christ in danger
Christ in hearts of all who love me
Christ in mouth of friend and stranger.

(67) STARTING WITH THE BIBLE

The Bible is the treasure store from which Christian devotion has always grown. If our prayer becomes distant from Scripture there will always be the danger that we lose our way in the jungle of our own prejudices or the 'undergrowth' of our own underdeveloped understanding of God. So how do we use the Bible in intercession?

1 **Reading the Bible** is a vital part of our time with God, and this will inevitably lead us to serious reflection on the truth behind the text and the applicability of the passage to our own life experience. Out of this encounter with the text, therefore, will come a desire to pray about many things – what we have seen afresh, what we need to do in response to the passage; or we may simply want to enjoy some profound truth we have rediscovered. But another response will very often be to intercede for someone we know to whom the passage seems to apply, or who has come to mind as we have thought about the passage. Follow your instinct on this, because God may often bring to the surface someone who is really in need of your love and prayer – when he's given a chance to do so!

2 **The Benedictine method** of meditation on Scripture offers a more structured and very helpful approach to this praying out of the Bible. In contemporary form the words to remember are *read – reflect – respond – rest*. We *read* the passage until a phrase hits us and asks for our attention. We then *reflect* on that phrase, chewing it over, thinking it through, tasting all the goodness, until it's yielded what it has to give us this time round. That leads us to *respond* in prayer, as above, and may lead us finally to *rest* in the presence of the God who has revealed himself to us afresh through his Word. We may then pick up the passage again and repeat the process.

3 **The Daily Office** has sustained the Church through the centuries, and all forms of it have the words of Scripture at the centre. These appear in the psalms, the canticles (sacred songs), the various responses, and in the readings from the Bible itself. Out of this Scripture-soaked experience comes the time for prayer at the end of the Office, and here again we will find that the encounter with Scripture is informing and guiding our praying and our intercession for others.

(68) FILES OF PRAYERS

*Two types of files may be particularly helpful as we take
intercession more seriously. Of course the very idea of a file
probably implies a certain kind of personality type – for some this
will be hopelessly over-organized! But simple variations may yet
prove helpful in enabling us to make the best use of our time
praying for others.*

A file of 'good' prayers

I've found it helpful over many years to accumulate in an A5 file
prayers which have particularly spoken to me. I may have come
across them in a service, or a book, or a magazine. They may
have turned up on a prayer card or a newsletter. I may even have
written some myself and not wanted to lose them! What makes
them valuable to me will be something to do with the images, the
use of ideas or words, the vivid way they pray out of sharp
situations, and many other things. And those factors will be
unique to me. But we then find that over time we have a treasury
of prayers which truly speak to us and for us. It would be one of
the first things I would rescue if the house were on fire!

A file for prayer

I'm not over-enthusiastic about lists for prayer. My heart sinks
when I see a long list of names of people for whom I should pray.
I know I can't sustain the spiritual or emotional energy to pray for
more than a few. And yet the needs are immense, and I receive
prayer letters and prayer diaries from all over. One answer is to
create your own file with different sections – marked by dividers –
for different needs.

The first section may be a sheet or sheets of file paper with the
names of: (1) Your family and closest friends who you are
committed in love to pray for. (2) Colleagues or more distant

145

acquaintances who you have heard about and want to hold before God. (3) Situations of seriousness or crisis which demand urgent, maybe short-term, prayer. This single sheet (or few sheets of small paper) could be replaced as regularly as wanted. It might become out of date, or it might be good to start with a new page at New Year or Lent, Easter and Advent. It should be fresh enough and short enough not to become daunting.

The second section may contain prayer diaries or prayer letters from those organizations or people who you are especially committed to support.

The third section may contain photographs of people you care for, or who you met on holiday and promised to remember, or the team of people you work with, or even your minister or bishop!

The fourth section may contain miscellaneous material such as maps of places in need, letters from special people, or newspaper cuttings about people and situations which have moved you and where you feel drawn to pray after the 'news machine' has moved on.

The value of this file is that you know from the start that you are not intending to pray for everything in it every day! You are therefore free to respond as the Spirit moves and to pray for different parts and different people and in different ways. You would probably always want to start with the list of people in the *first section*, but after that would be free to move with your inclination. This kind of file can make intercession interesting and varied rather than a duty and a drudge.

A very small file

If the whole idea of a file is infinitely depressing, it may yet be worth considering having a very small file or notebook in which there is a different name on each page. You can then pray for as many pages/people as you want without being overwhelmed by the number of names before you. Simple!

(69) MIND-MAPPING

Mind-mapping is a familiar tool for learning and analysing information, but it can also be used helpfully in personal intercession. Instead of using lists, files and other 'left-brain', linear models, mind-mapping involves covering a blank sheet of paper with images and connections between different prayer needs. It's a visual representation of who and what you are praying for, and allows you to see at a single glance the extent of your prayer commitments.

An example

You may put in the centre of your sheet of paper (either A4 or larger) the names of your family and closest friends or even 'stick-people' with names attached. Out to the right of the paper you may draw an outline church and put there a number of the names or projects that you are praying for. Beneath that you may depict another clump of interests – social concerns, charities, overseas projects which you support, and you might draw a line connecting the church with these concerns because it's through the local church that you got involved with many of them.

Out to the left you may have two clusters of people – friends and people in special need, maybe linked. Elsewhere you may depict the local school with which you are much involved, and a name or two attached. There may be another part of the map which has space for groups and people in the local community, your workplace and leisure groups. Connecting lines may or may not be used to make relevant links. A globe may reflect your commitment to pray for world events or environmental issues.

And so the mind-map is built up. In your time of prayer you can then lay the map out and pray over it, focusing on particular parts and people as you feel led that day. You can add to the map at any time, and restart it when it becomes too complex. When you draw the map afresh, one of the liberating features of this way of praying is that you can start with a completely different presentation of your 'world' of intercession; you don't have to start with the same areas in the same place. Moreover, you can use different colours; you can put stars by urgent needs, or photos by particular people. The whole approach is much more appealing to people who think visually and systemically, and may be worth trying sometimes even by boring, 'left-brain', linear thinkers like me!

(70) THE LORD'S PRAYER

*The Lord's own prayer is immensely rich, presenting us with
material to reflect on and pray with for a lifetime. One of its
greatest strengths is that if we are going through a dry period and
aren't sure how to pray, we know that in this prayer is the heart
of the matter – we're returning to the 'gold standard' in prayer.
Here are a few ways of using this glorious prayer to help our own
prayer and intercession.*

(a) The pregnant pause

This prayer is said millions of times a day, but for many of us,
our concentration on what we're praying isn't all it might be!
We're too used to it. One way of addressing this problem is to
pause on a different phrase each day for a week and to pray
that phrase from the heart. Finally we repeat the phrase and
continue with the rest of the prayer. It means we have the
chance to inhabit the prayer, to fill it out, to let it lead us
further and deeper. And that phrase can then be our companion
phrase for the day. Sunday: Our Father in heaven; Monday:
hallowed be your name; Tuesday: your kingdom come, and so
on. This 'pausing' can also be done in a small group: for
instance, in a house group, or by people saying the daily office
together.

(b) Full immersion

A group of students were once asked by their tutor to go away
and pray the Lord's Prayer all afternoon – a full three hours. They
were bemused; how could they stretch it out? When they returned
to their tutor they said they'd run out of time to pray it all
through! It can be a good experience to be fully immersed in the
Lord's Prayer in this way. We discover how much is contained in
each phrase; we experience the balance of praise, prayer for the
world and prayer for ourselves; we feel the depth of our Lord's

149

insight into prayer and into human need. Take time – sometime – to pray this prayer by full immersion.

(c) Like the Jesus Prayer

Just as the Orthodox 'Jesus prayer' is often repeated, again and again, in the rhythm of the person's breathing, so the Lord's Prayer can be used as a way of getting to the heart of the One who gave the prayer. We can repeat it calmly, without haste, until it becomes almost second nature. We can do it while walking, driving, or simply sitting still. It undoubtedly takes discipline to settle into this rhythmic form of prayer but the effect can be profound as we increasingly centre our lives on the Lord, the Giver of Life.

(d) The artistic response

How about setting yourself the task, when you have more time, of responding to the Lord's Prayer in some artistic form? This could be with modelling clay – it's extraordinary what comes out of our often-captive creativity when we get the chance. Or we could paint a response or do some creative writing or poetry. What about a personal letter to God, arising out of thorough engagement with the prayer? We can all do so much more than we ever think!

(71) HOT-SPOTS

When we come to pray it can be a good exercise to look back
over the last 24 hours and re-run the main events. This will
include the people we've met, the jobs we've done, the meetings
we've been to, the leisure activities and so on. As we run over
these events in the context of prayer it's like having a spiritual
Geiger counter in operation, and some events will prove to be
more 'excitable' than others. These are the hot-spots which call us
to special prayer. It may be that we remember the particular pain
or weariness of somebody at a meeting. It may be that we became
very aware of the needs of an organization or the problematic
dynamics of a family. There may be someone we simply want to
thank God for and for whom we ask God's continuing blessing.

Our day-by-day experience of life isn't an undifferentiated
chronicle of events; it's a rich story of varying textures and hues.
Praying over our experience like this allows the Spirit to direct
our thoughts and prayers to the places of most significance. But
we have to have the Geiger counter turned on!

(72) A HANDFUL OF PRAYERS

You probably feel that there are too many people for whom you should be praying. Take heart! Jesus seems to have prayed for particular people as they presented themselves with their needs. He may well have prayed more generally for the peace of the world, and surely he prayed for the hosts of people who were turning up to see him, but the only evidence we have is that he prayed one by one.

Maybe we can extend that to praying for a handful of people at any one time. Perhaps in our morning prayers we can identify the five or ten people we feel most bound to pray for (five is usually fine for me) and then carry them around during the day. That's our 'handful of prayers'. Then during the day, when we notice our hand at rest on our knee or holding a cup of tea or operating a keyboard, that might remind us of our five people, and in the very act of noticing and remembering, our prayer for them is renewed. In that way, we 'pray without ceasing' for these special folk.

(73) LIGHTING A CANDLE

The power of lighting candles is well known in most religious
traditions. There are many references to candles in this book, not
least in lighting one at the start of a time of prayer to mark it out
as a time given to God. But there are times when we are praying
for someone and it helps simply to light a special candle for them,
letting the continuing flame represent our desire to maintain our
prayer for them. This, of course, is the basis of the well-
established practice of lighting candles in churches for special
needs; why should we not do the same at home? When our
daughters had left home and were facing challenging situations
with exams, interviews and the like, I would often come home to
find a candle burning on my wife's desk beside her as she worked.
The prayer was continuing.

(74) LETTERS, PHONE CALLS, EMAILS

Without becoming too pious about it, here is a wonderful
opportunity to pray for the people we have dealings with. When
we sign a letter to someone, it takes but a moment – indeed
simply a thought – to commend to God the person to whom
we're sending the letter. God doesn't need lots of agonized prayer
on our part in order to receive our intercession; merely the
intention will do. The same applies to emails, although the
impersonal nature of a keyboard makes it more difficult than
when we're personally signing our name. With time and gentle
discipline even email can be used to the glory of God!

Similarly with the phone. There's a moment when we've put the
receiver down when we haven't yet moved on to the next activity
or gone back to the one from which we were interrupted. This is
a moment when we could conceivably pray for the person to
whom we've been talking. Again, the day doesn't need to be
interspersed with heavy times of intercession; simply holding that
person before God for a moment will do. You may not feel like
doing this with all callers!

(75) PRAYING FOR THOSE YOU FORGET!

One of the things that can make Christians feel most guilty is not praying for people for whom we have promised to pray. I've felt worst of all when someone has come up and thanked me for my prayers (which have apparently been wonderfully effective!) when I know full well that I haven't really prayed at all. Sometimes we feel obliged to promise to pray. Sometimes people ask us at a moment when we can't jot it down. At other times we just aren't motivated. At other times we simply forget.

So what's to be done? The first thing is to let ourselves off the hook of guilt. Guilt of this kind rarely does any good. Life is full and complex and we simply can't deliver all we would like. The second thing is to remember the wise advice of Michael Ramsey to send an immediate arrow prayer for this person or need, even if in many cases that was it as far as prayer was concerned. But behind that is a deeper and more liberating truth. When we come before God in prayer we come with everything we are and everything we're carrying. Part of that is the fact that we were asked to pray for so-and-so and forgot. God can handle that. He takes the intention of the heart to pray for that person and it's enough. If our prayer depended on the fullness of our information, or the accuracy of our theology, or the fluency of our expression, we'd get nowhere. All God wants is our desire to pray. Indeed all God wants is *us*, just us, with all we are. So we can be sure that when we come to him with our forgotten prayers, he'll be able to find them, and he won't forget.

What a relief!

FURTHER RESOURCES

These books have their focus on intercession in particular, not on prayer in general.

General collections

Angela Ashwin (ed.), *The Book of a Thousand Prayers*. Zondervan 2002.
Mary Batchelor (ed.), *The Lion Prayer Collection*. Lion 1992.
Frank Colquhoun, *Parish Prayers, New Parish Prayers, Contemporary Parish Prayers*. Hodder and Stoughton paperbacks 1999/2000.
Robin Keeley (ed.), *Prayers Encircling the World*. SPCK 1998.
Colin Podmore (ed.), *Prayers to Remember*. DLT 2001.
The SPCK Book of Christian Prayer. SPCK 1995.

Public worship

David Adam, *Clouds of Glory, Traces of Glory, Glimpses of Glory*. SPCK 1998, 1999, 2000.
Nick Fawcett, *Selected Prayers for Public Worship*. Kevin Mayhew 2003.
Christine Odell, *Companion to the Revised Common Lectionary: Intercessions*. Epworth 1998.
John Pritchard, *The Intercessions Handbook*. SPCK 1997.
Susan Sayers, *Prayers of Intercession*. Kevin Mayhew 2000.
Eric Simmons, *Look with Mercy*. Mirfield 2003.
Raymond Williams, *Leading Intercessions*. Canterbury Press 2000.
Raymond Williams, *Hear our Prayer*. Canterbury Press 2003.

Informal worship and small groups

Geoffrey Duncan, *Seeing Christ in Others*. Canterbury Press 2002.
Kathy Galloway, *The Pattern of our Days*. Wild Goose 1996.
Janet Morley (ed.), *Bread of Tomorrow: Praying with the World's Poor*. SPCK 2004.
Susan Sayers, *God's People at Worship Together*. Kevin Mayhew 2003.
Wild Goose Worship Group, *A Wee Worship Book*. Wild Goose 1999.

Children and young people

Nick Aitken, *Prayers for Teenagers*. SPCK 2003.
Nick Aitken and Tim Sudworth, *At the Cutting Edge*. Canterbury Press 2003.
Nick Aitken and Rowan Williams, *Family Prayers*. SPCK 2002.
Jonny Baker and Doug Gay, *Alternative Worship*. SPCK 2003.
Robert Cooper, *A World of Wonders*. SPCK 2003.
Katie Thompson, *Intercessions for Young People*. Kevin Mayhew 2001.

Personal prayer

David Adam, *The Edge of Glory, Tides and Seasons, The Open Gate*. SPCK 1985, 1989, 1994.
Eddie Askew, *A Silence and a Shouting, Disguises of Love, Facing the Storm*. Leprosy Mission 1982, 1983, 1989.
Nick Fawcett, *Daily Prayer*. Kevin Mayhew 2000.
John Pritchard, *How to Pray*. SPCK 2002.
Frank Topping (ed.), *Daily Prayer*. Oxford University Press 2003.

Theology of intercession

Peter Baelz, *Does God Answer Prayer?* DLT 1982.
Tim Gorringe, *God's Theatre: A Theology of Providence*. SCM Press 1991.
John Polkinghorne, *Science and Providence*. SPCK 1989.
Fraser Watts (ed.), *Perspectives on Prayer*. SPCK 2001.
Vernon White, *The Fall of a Sparrow*. Paternoster 1985.